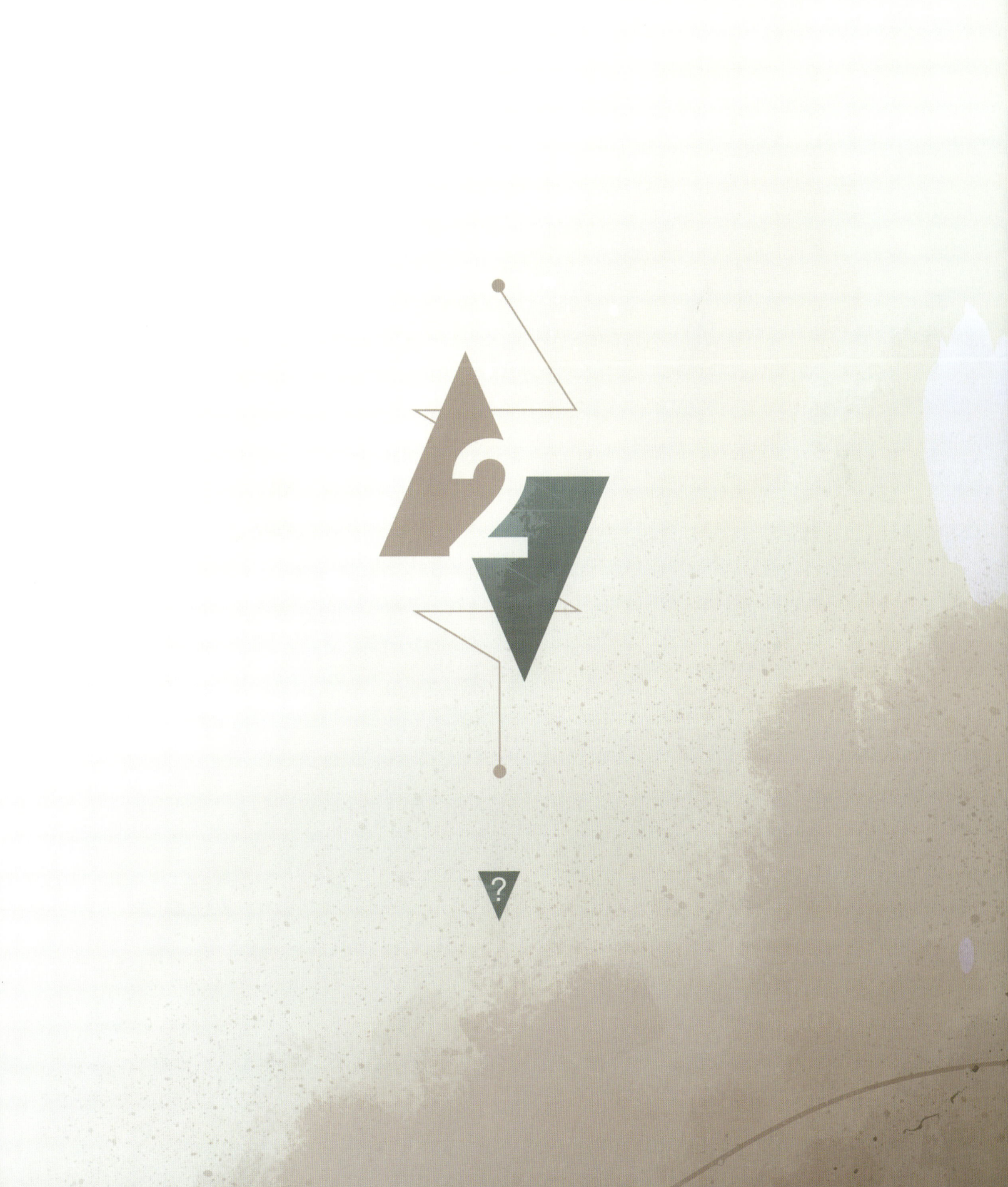

The more you get pushed into corner, the more you can also find hidden forms
and hidden architectures...
                    - The Brothers Quay

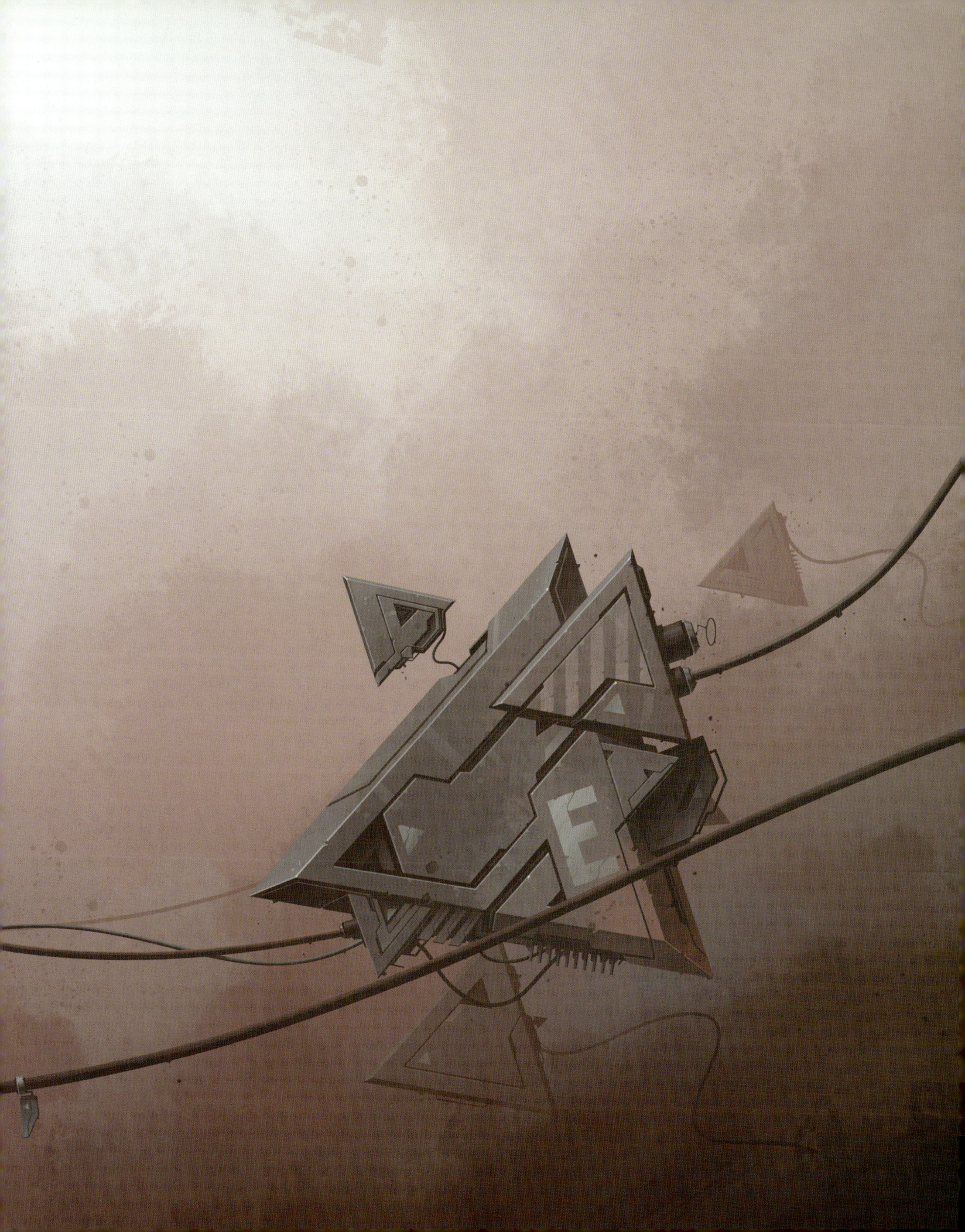

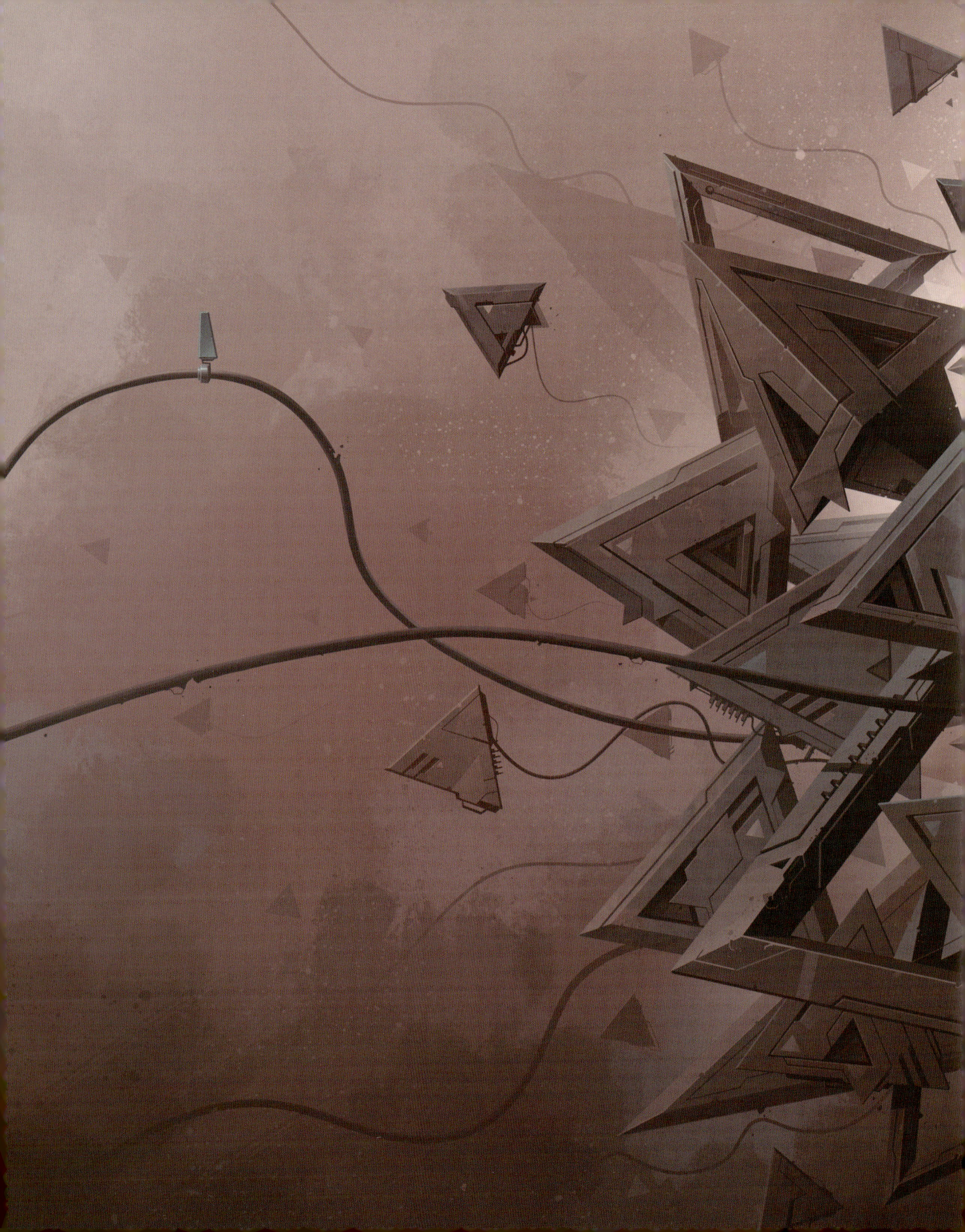

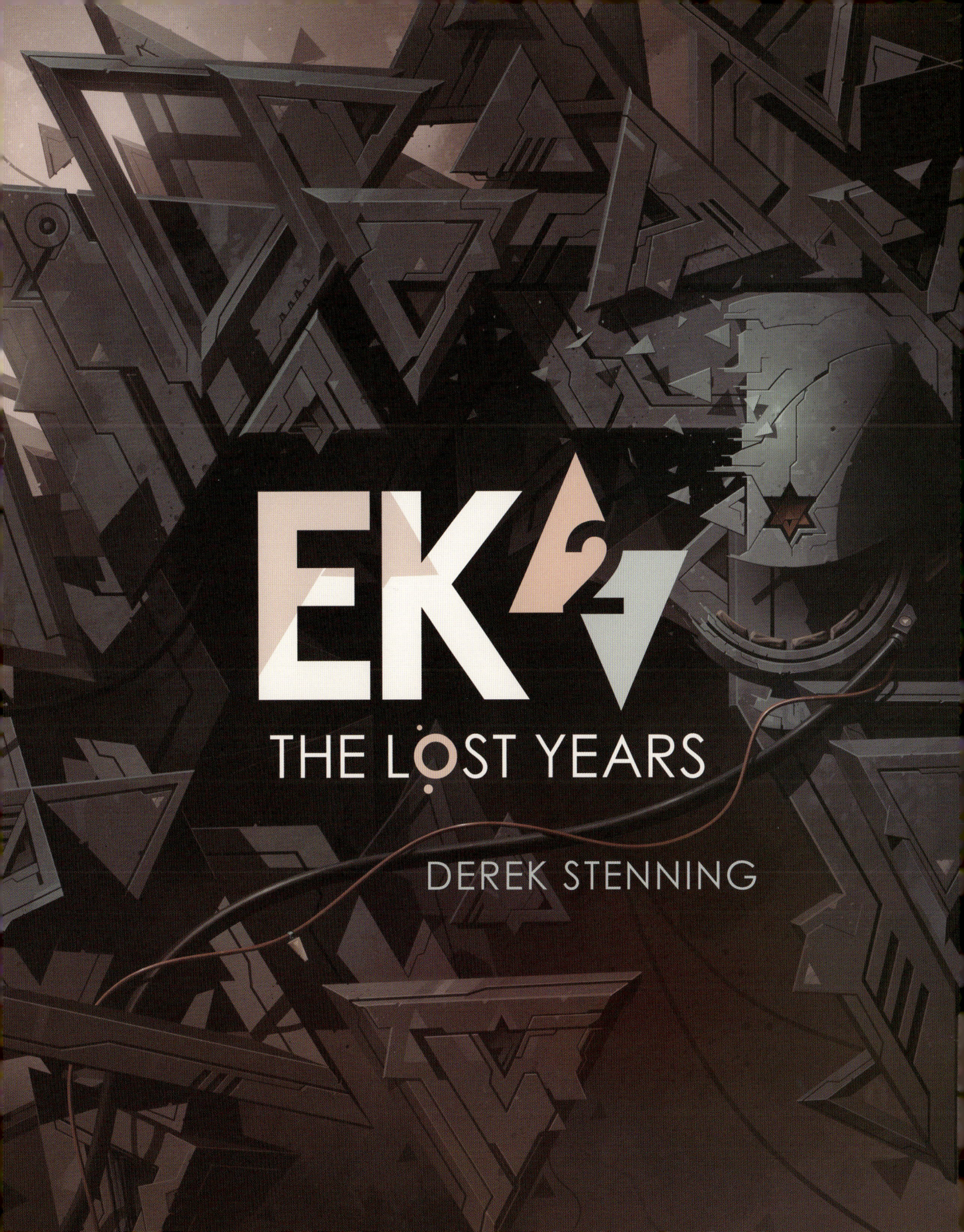

EK2 - The Lost Years
Created by Derek Stenning
borninconcrete.com
derek@borninconcrete.com

Book Design & Production Layout: Derek Stenning
Copy Editor: Sara DeGonia
Photography Credits: Ownage, Ax2 Limited, Michael Fichtenmayer,
Lesley Stenning
Model Renders: Gene Campbell, Leo Haslam

Published by Design Studio Press
www.designstudiopress.com
info@designstudiopress.com

10 9 8 7 6 5 4 3 2 1

Printed in China
First Edition, 2022

Library Of Congress Control Number: 2022935325

ISBN-13: 978-162465070-3

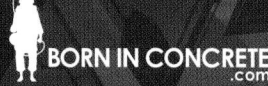

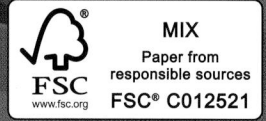

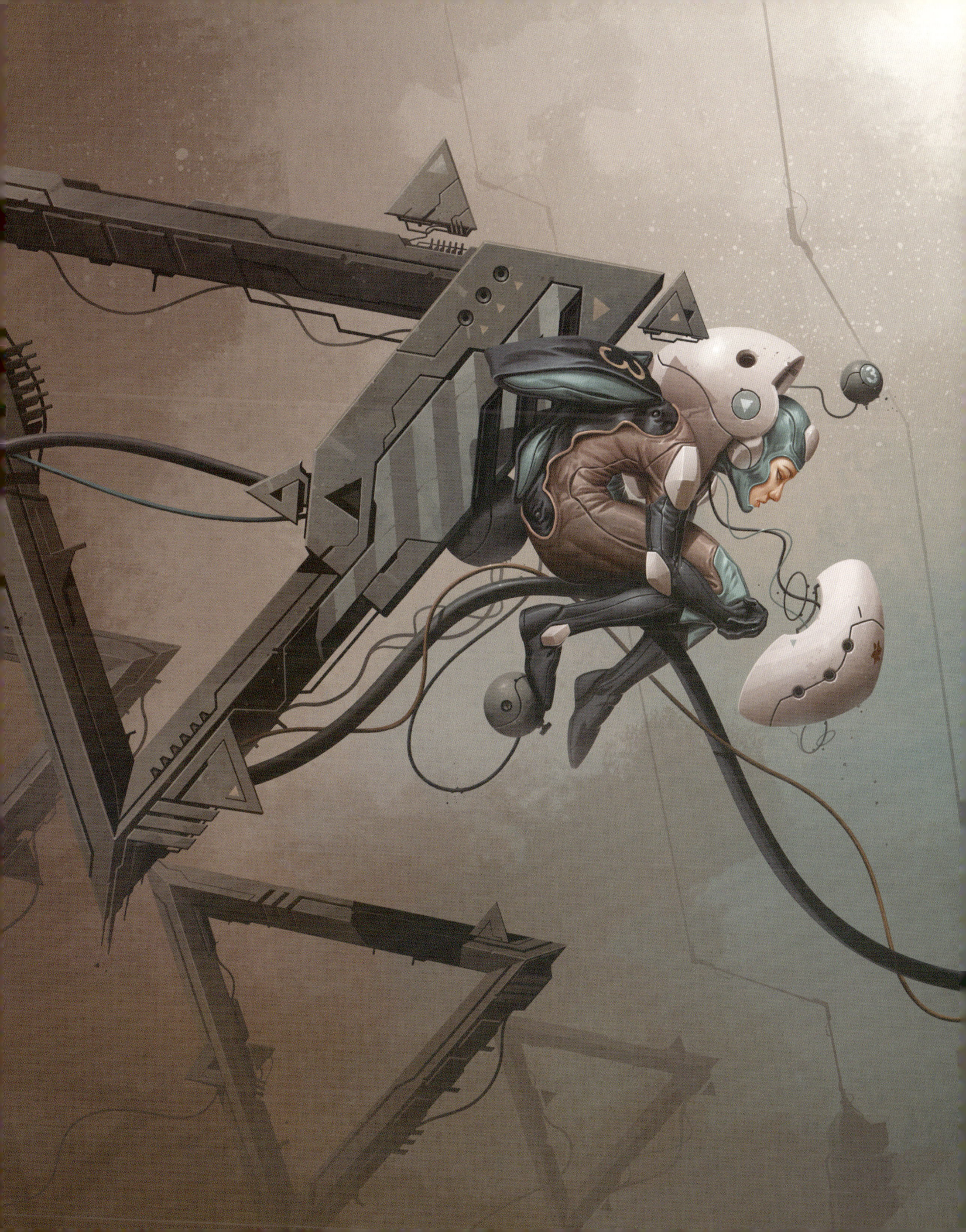

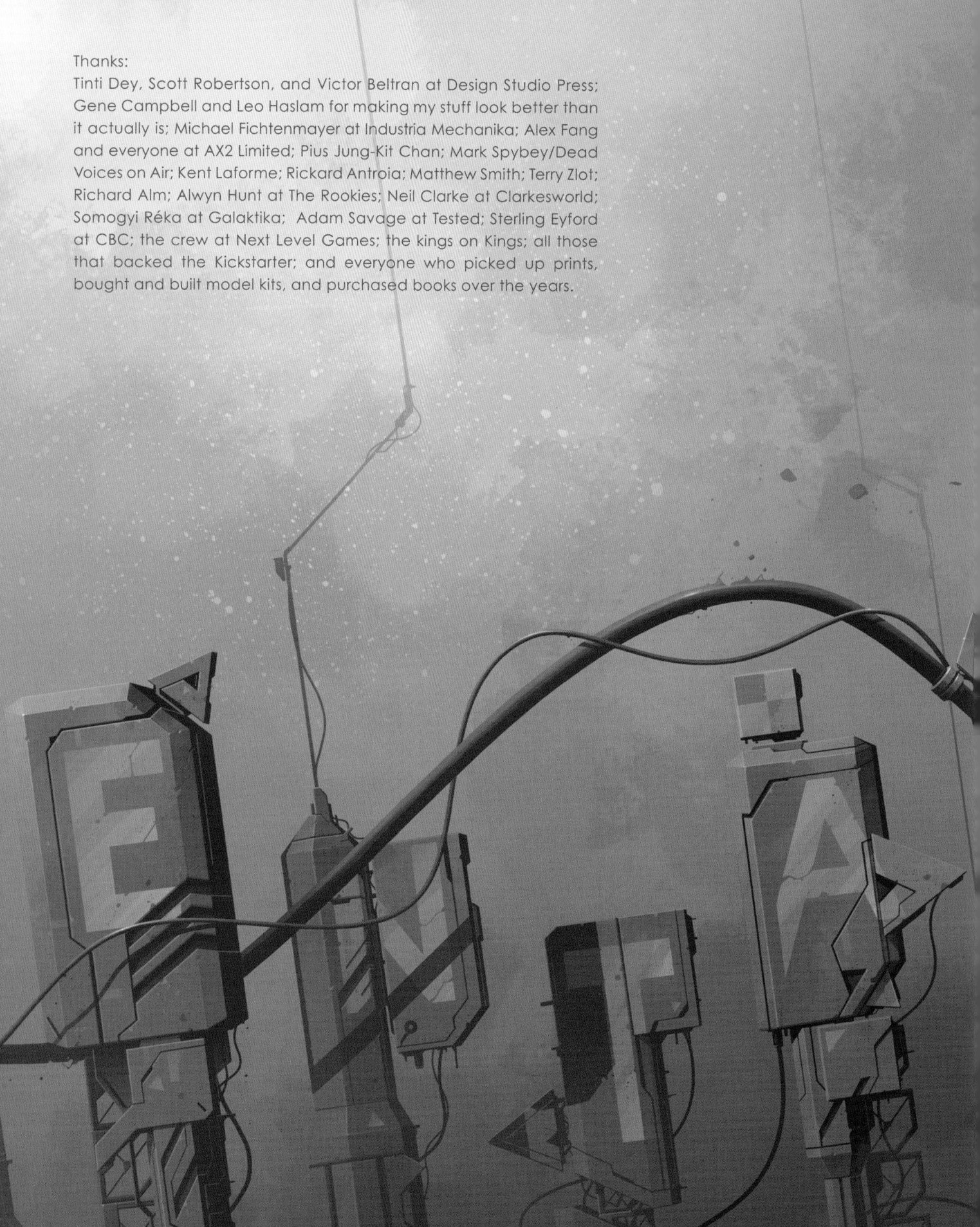

Thanks:

Tinti Dey, Scott Robertson, and Victor Beltran at Design Studio Press; Gene Campbell and Leo Haslam for making my stuff look better than it actually is; Michael Fichtenmayer at Industria Mechanika; Alex Fang and everyone at AX2 Limited; Pius Jung-Kit Chan; Mark Spybey/Dead Voices on Air; Kent Laforme; Rickard Antroia; Matthew Smith; Terry Zlot; Richard Alm; Alwyn Hunt at The Rookies; Neil Clarke at Clarkesworld; Somogyi Réka at Galaktika; Adam Savage at Tested; Sterling Eyford at CBC; the crew at Next Level Games; the kings on Kings; all those that backed the Kickstarter; and everyone who picked up prints, bought and built model kits, and purchased books over the years.

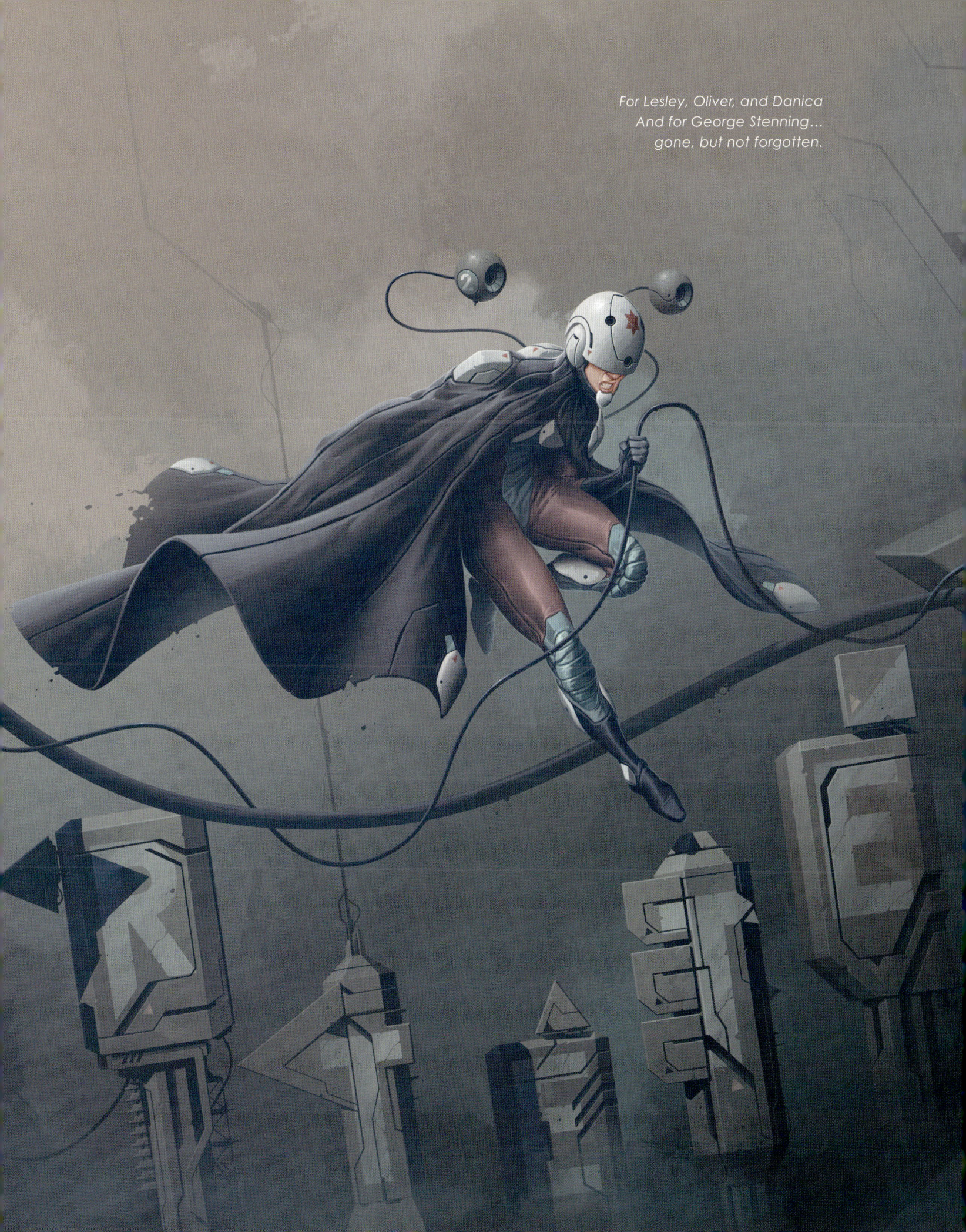

For Lesley, Oliver, and Danica
And for George Stenning...
gone, but not forgotten.

CONTENTS

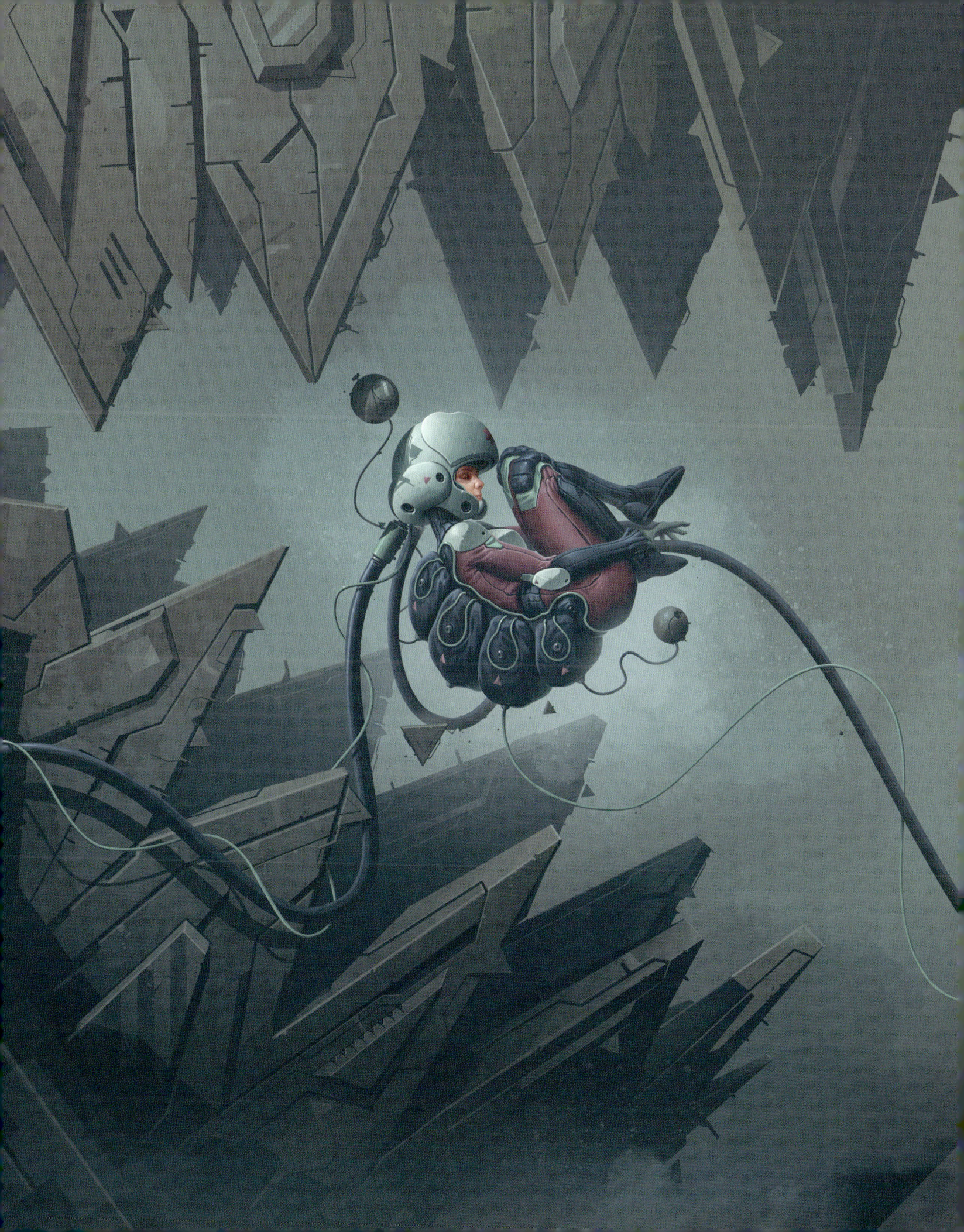

THE LOST YEARS

These last few years have been challenging, particularly from a personal work point of view, and a lot of this time seems lost to me. After I finished the first EK Series art book I had planned to move onto other creative projects that had been in my head for a while. Unfortunately, and as is often the case, life intervened and during the proceeding years it would be a struggle to find the time, the energy and the direction to work on any personal projects at all.

It started with a studio closure, which left me wondering what I was going to do to support my family. I overcompensated and took on multiple jobs. One was a regular 30-hours-per-week gig. This left me with time in my week to do additional freelance work, so I often made sure that I had another project going. Rarely did this additional work fit nicely into an extra 10 hours a week - usually more like 15, sometimes 20, or even 25 extra hours. It was also pretty consistent, as there always seemed to be another project on the horizon. So, working 50 to 55 hours per week, while having a family with two kids and other commitments, left little time to do my own artwork. The upside, of course, was that it was great financially, but I foolishly fell into the "money trap" as our lifestyle increased along with our increased resources. Soon we were off to live in France and travel around Europe for a year. This was a wonderful experience, especially for the kids, but it was busy - working two gigs for a decent chunk of the time we were away, combined with the amount of travelling, left me drained both creatively and physically.

cont. p.14

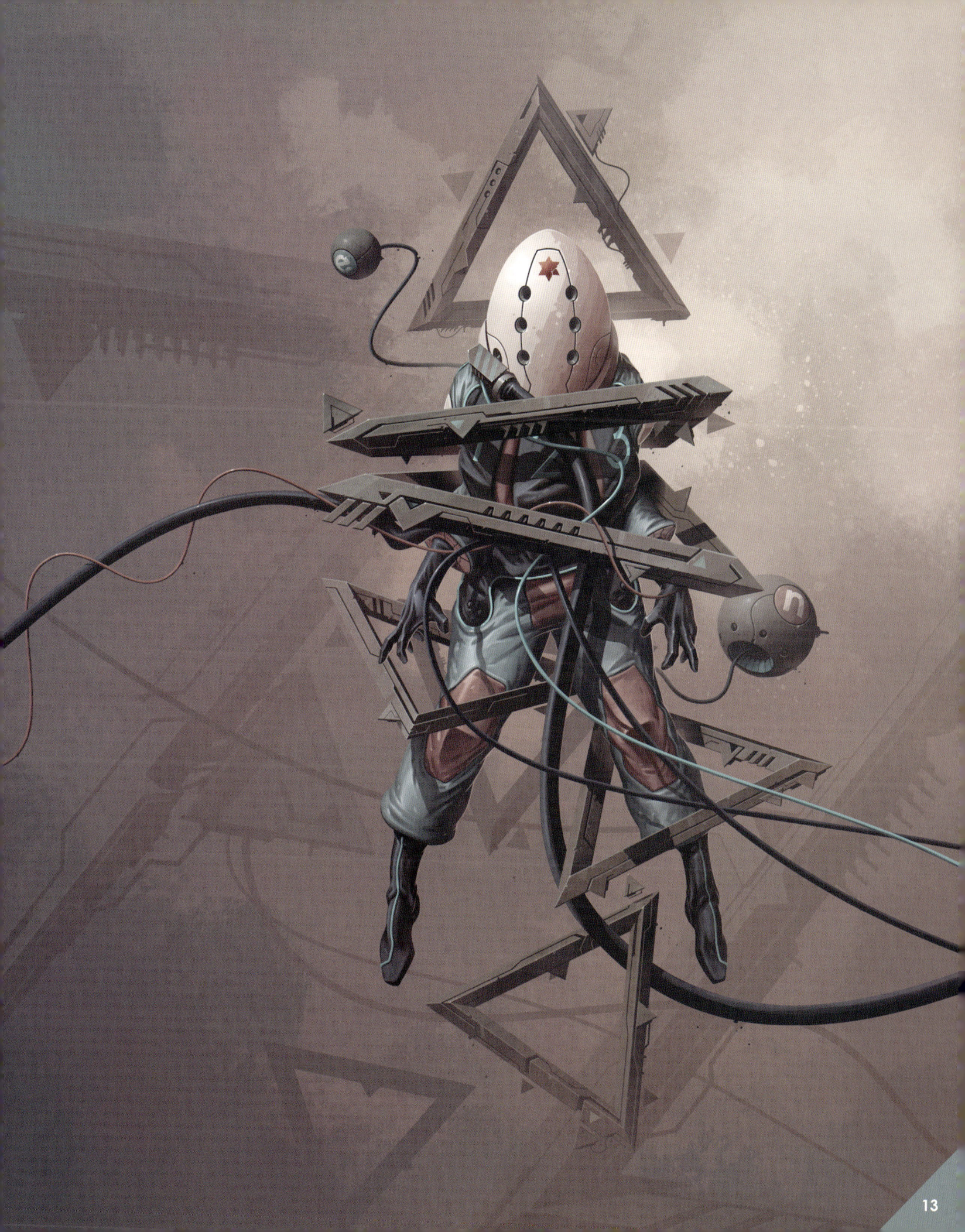

cont. from p.12

When we returned to Canada, we discovered that the tenants who had been renting our place had turned our house into a peanut butter factory (that's another story), and I needed to completely clean the place out and do some repairs.

Then there was my Dad. While we were still living in Europe, my cousin told me that my Dad had started acting a little strangely. Once we returned, it immediately became apparent that something was wrong, and within a few weeks he was diagnosed with vascular dementia. During the next year, as my father's dementia advanced, I increasingly became his caregiver. By spring 2017 I had to cut out all additional freelance work as the demands of taking care of my dad grew. He had pushed away all friends and family and refused to have outside help come in to assist him. By the end of 2017, and into early 2018, I was spending most days with my dad, and then coming home to be with my family, before working late into the night. It was a situation that was physically and mentally exhausting, and it was unsustainable.

Right when I was at the breaking point, in a moment of clarity, my father agreed to move into one of the care facilities that I had lined up for him. This was a huge relief. But dementia care is expensive. So now I had to clear out his house of 50 years and prepare it to sell, so, if need be, he could afford the care he needed for many years to come.

Once all this was settled, I was looking for some time off, but for various reasons, I ended up taking on more work. I was soon working on two projects again, and three months later my wife sustained an injury that left her bedridden and in rehabilitation for several months. It wasn't until early 2019 that I pared down to one project again and things began to settle down in my personal life. I had some space to breathe.

With this breathing room I could reflect on the last few years. In all the stress, within all the burnout and busy times, I had always turned back to my Entartete Kunst, or EK Series work. There were many pieces that I had worked on over the years to blow off steam and get me through. Most were just rough sketches, and very few were finished. They were started and left, as I had no time to complete them. During this time of reflection, a couple projects presented themselves that compelled me to dive back into the EK work. So, I had the idea to take these rough pieces that I had created over the years and finish them off. There were still hiccups, of course, but I had a renewed commitment to finish the work I started. Hopefully, by completing this work, by creating this book, in some way this will allow me, from an artistic point of view, to reclaim these lost years.

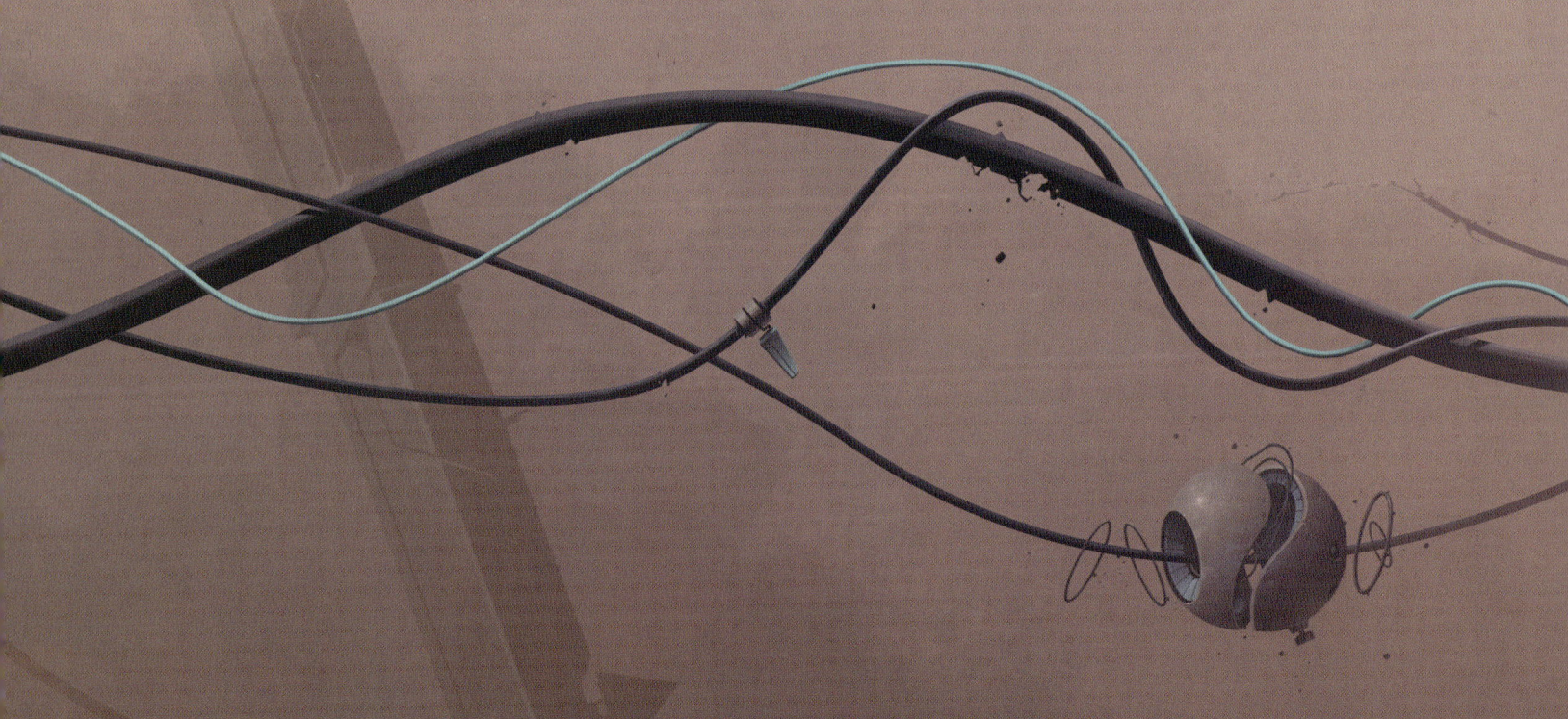

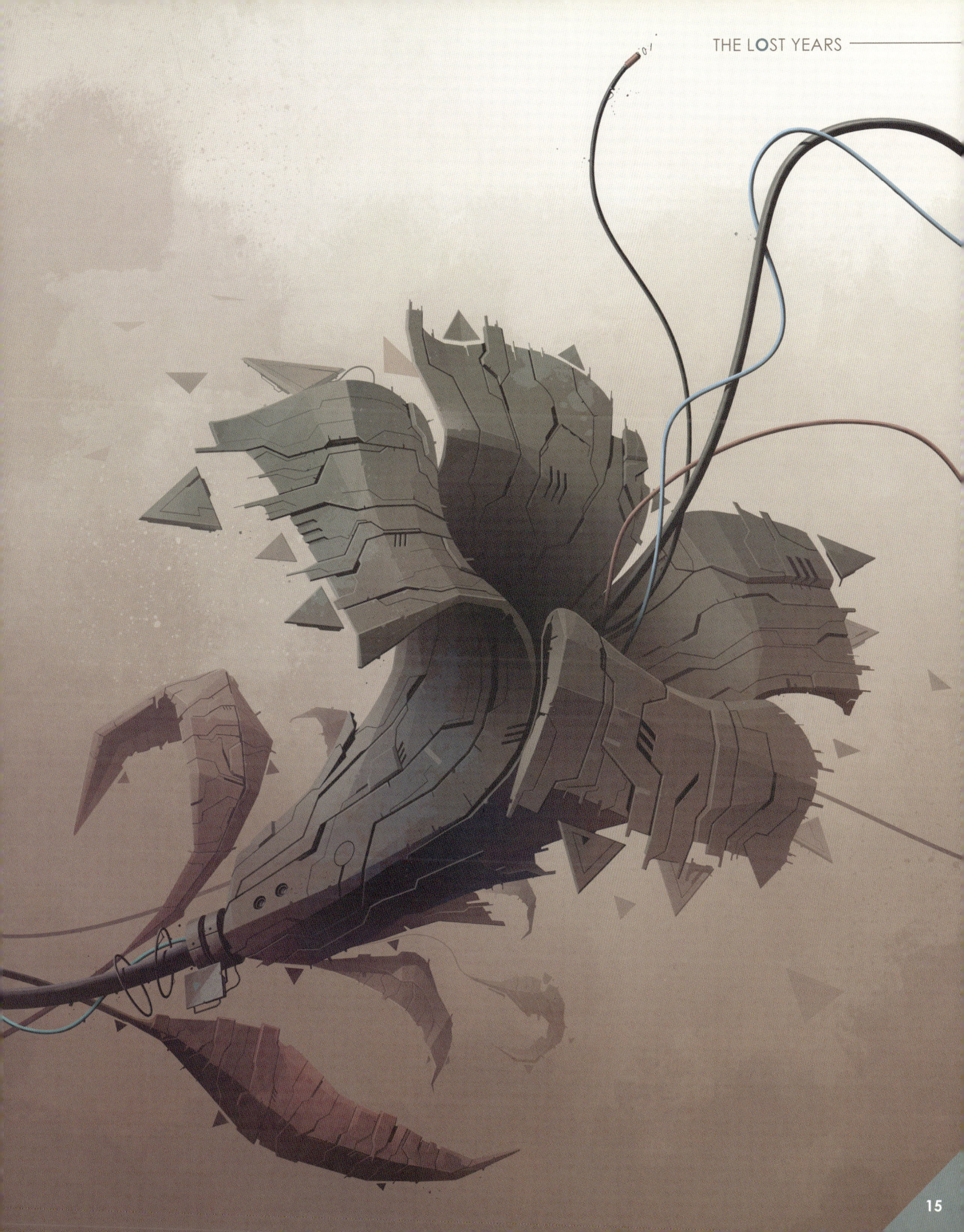

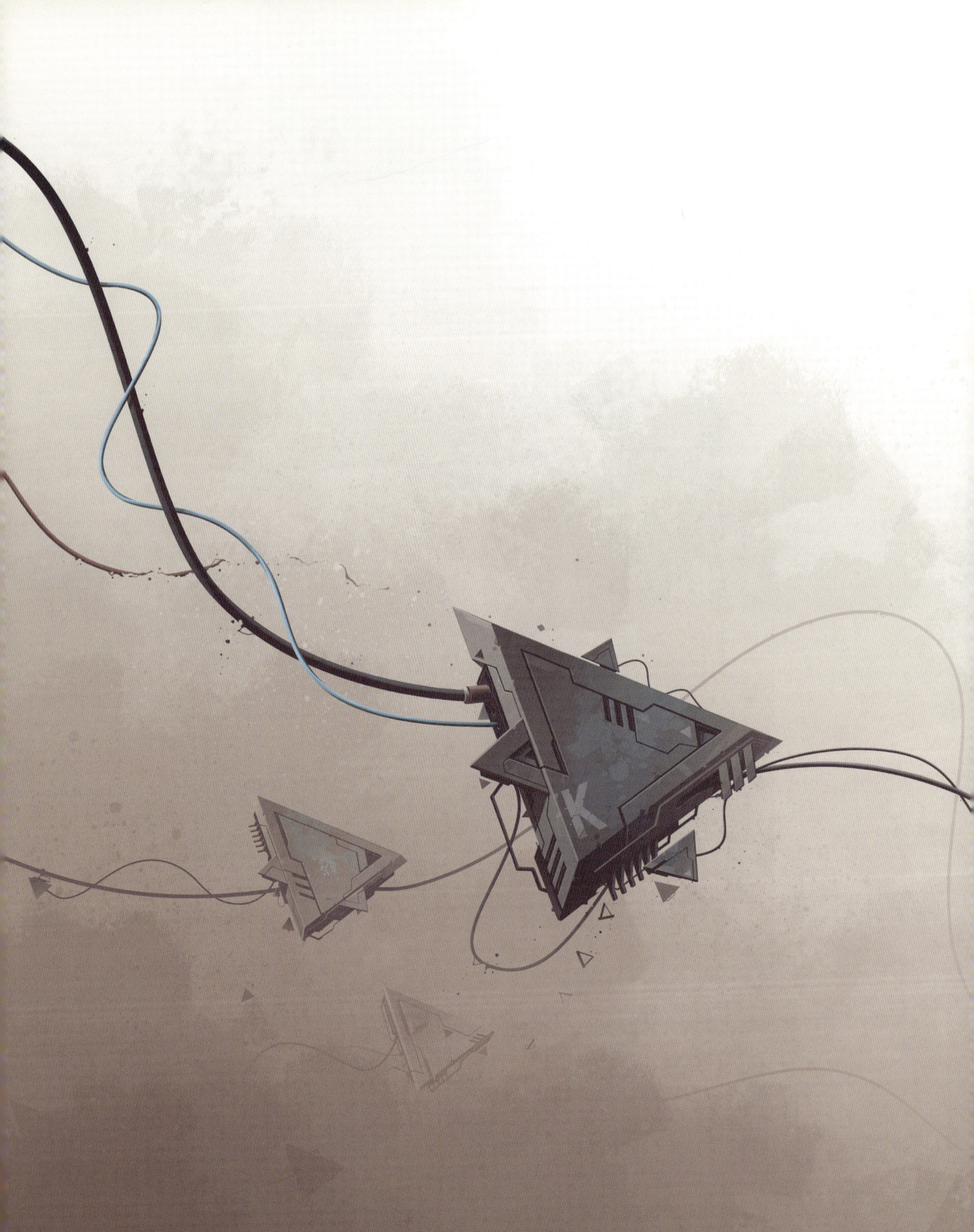

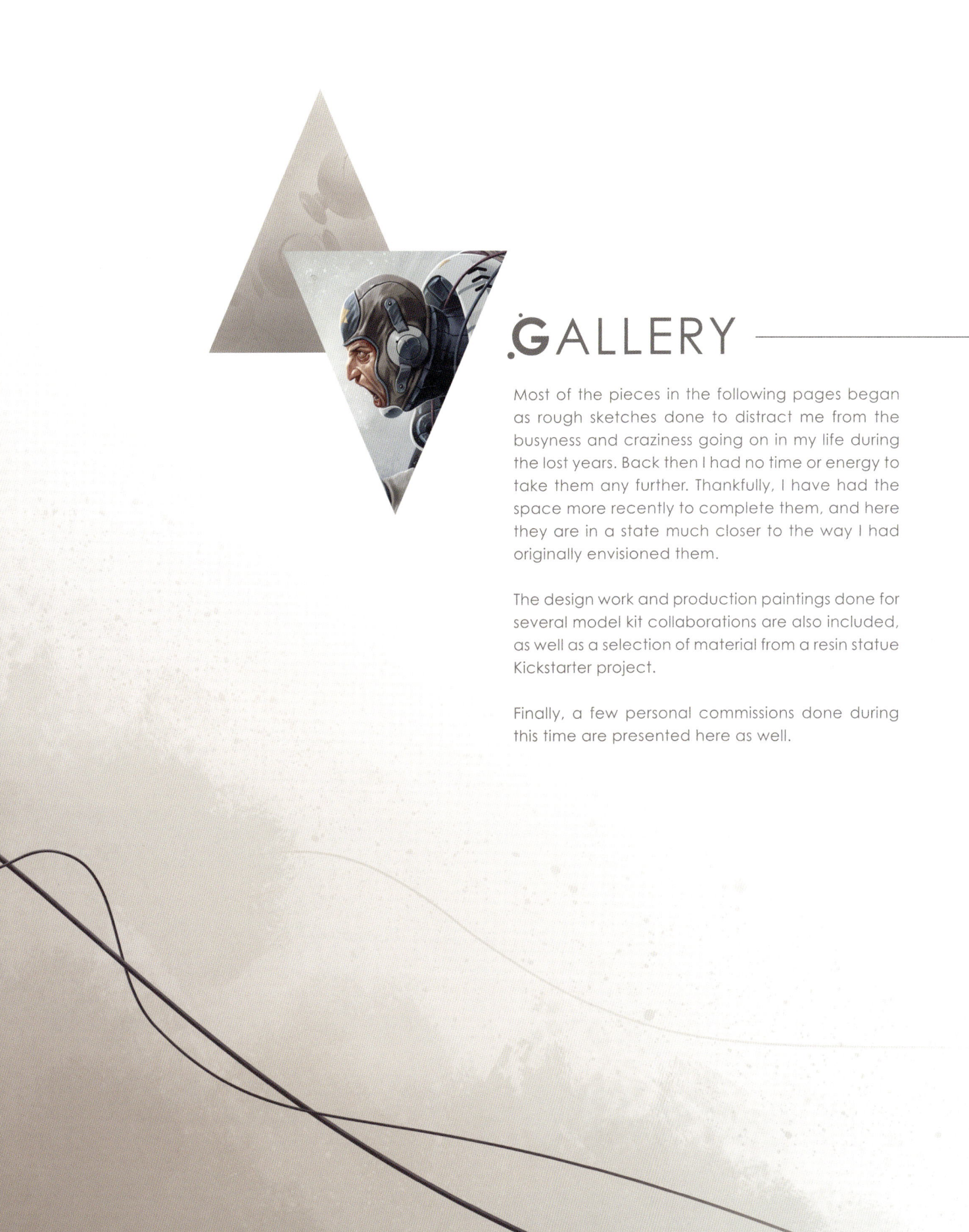

GALLERY

Most of the pieces in the following pages began as rough sketches done to distract me from the busyness and craziness going on in my life during the lost years. Back then I had no time or energy to take them any further. Thankfully, I have had the space more recently to complete them, and here they are in a state much closer to the way I had originally envisioned them.

The design work and production paintings done for several model kit collaborations are also included, as well as a selection of material from a resin statue Kickstarter project.

Finally, a few personal commissions done during this time are presented here as well.

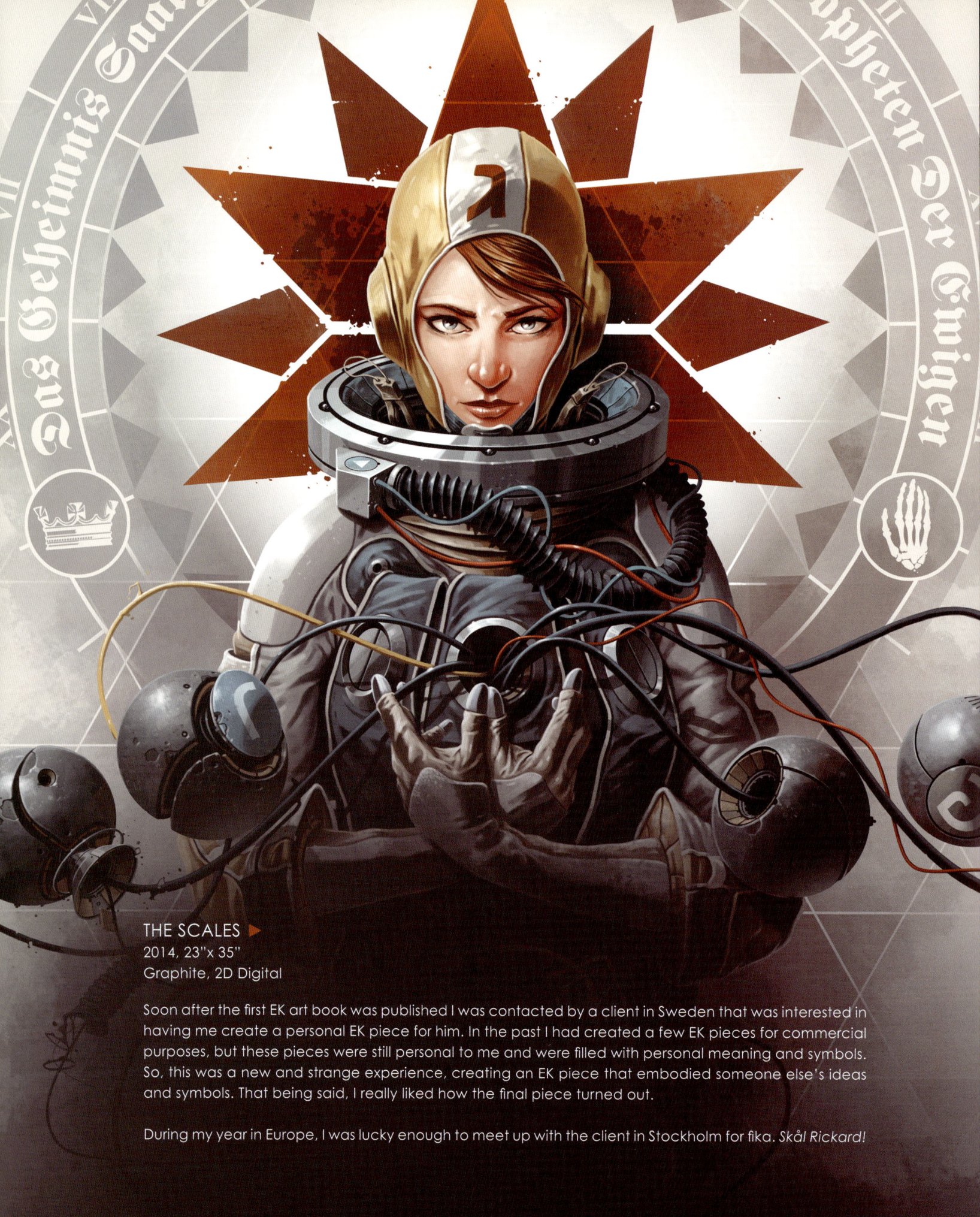

THE SCALES ▶
2014, 23"x 35"
Graphite, 2D Digital

Soon after the first EK art book was published I was contacted by a client in Sweden that was interested in having me create a personal EK piece for him. In the past I had created a few EK pieces for commercial purposes, but these pieces were still personal to me and were filled with personal meaning and symbols. So, this was a new and strange experience, creating an EK piece that embodied someone else's ideas and symbols. That being said, I really liked how the final piece turned out.

During my year in Europe, I was lucky enough to meet up with the client in Stockholm for fika. *Skål Rickard!*

EK[R]

die waage

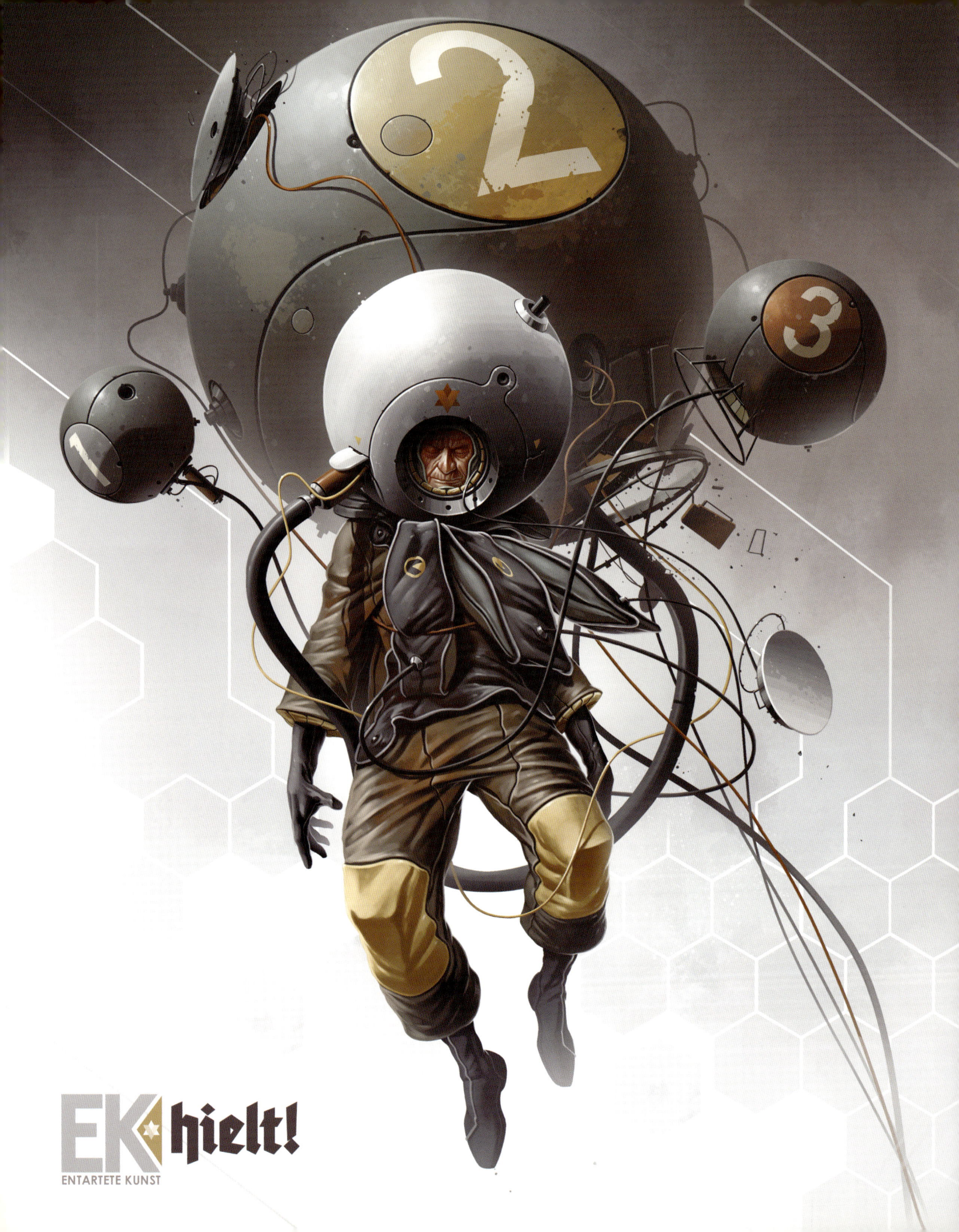

EK ★ hielt!
ENTARTETE KUNST

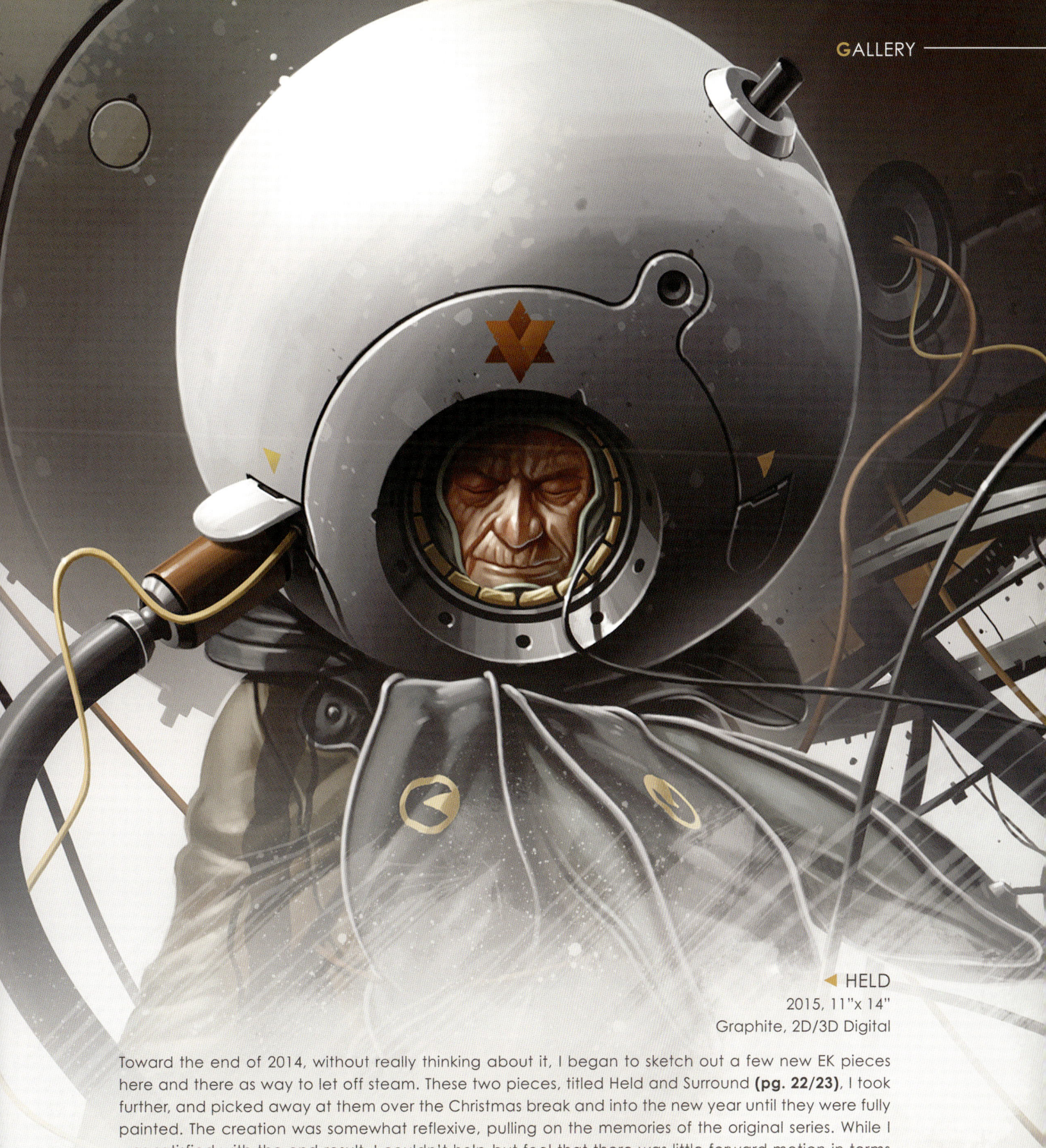

◄ HELD
2015, 11"x 14"
Graphite, 2D/3D Digital

Toward the end of 2014, without really thinking about it, I began to sketch out a few new EK pieces here and there as way to let off steam. These two pieces, titled Held and Surround **(pg. 22/23)**, I took further, and picked away at them over the Christmas break and into the new year until they were fully painted. The creation was somewhat reflexive, pulling on the memories of the original series. While I was satisfied with the end result, I couldn't help but feel that there was little forward motion in terms of artistic progression. The titles are references to this feeling, the feeling of being surrounded or stuck, being held in one place. In my case, I was overloaded with work with little or no time to develop or pursue new artistic endeavours, and retreating back to the comfort of the EK Series.

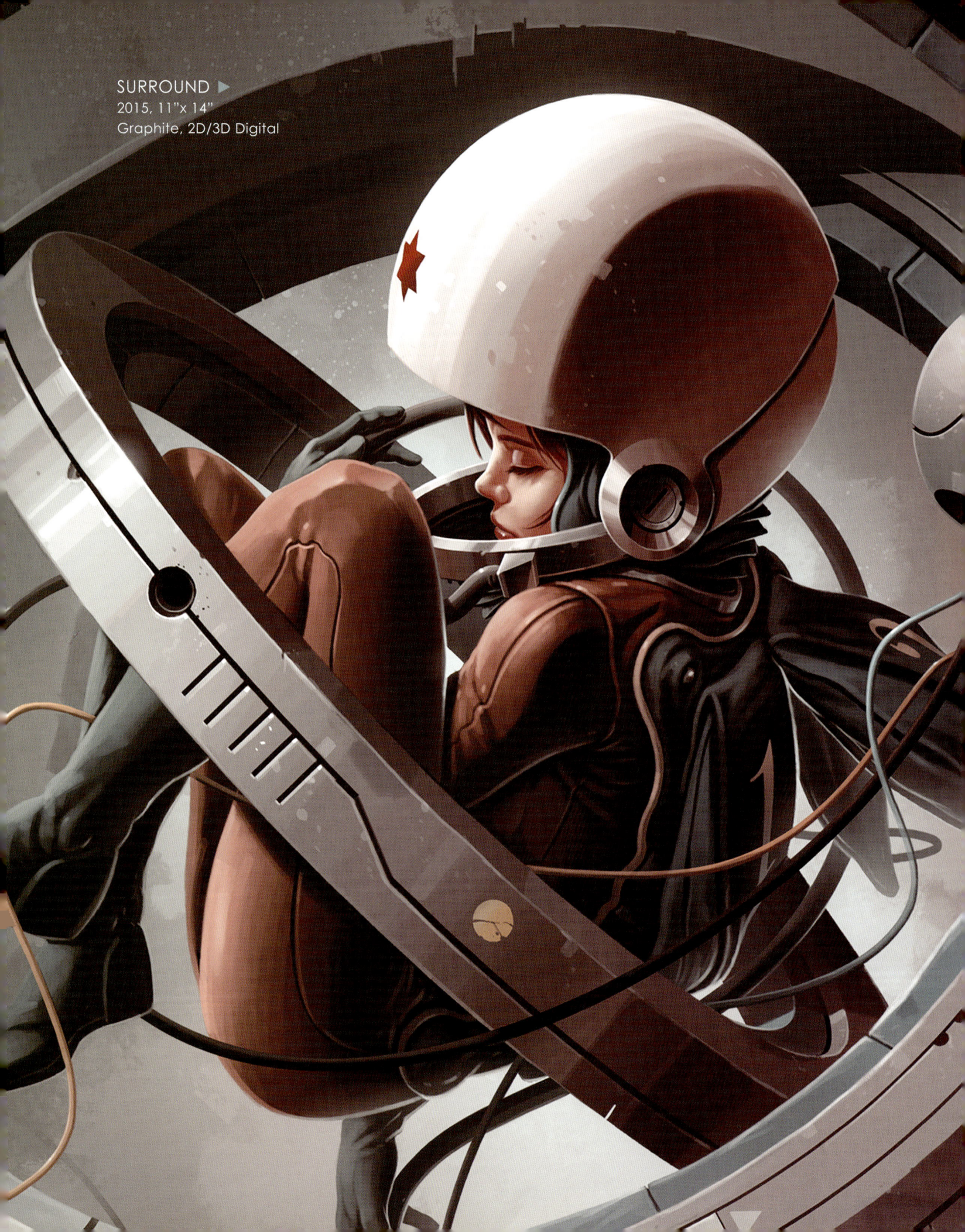

SURROUND ▶
2015, 11"x 14"
Graphite, 2D/3D Digital

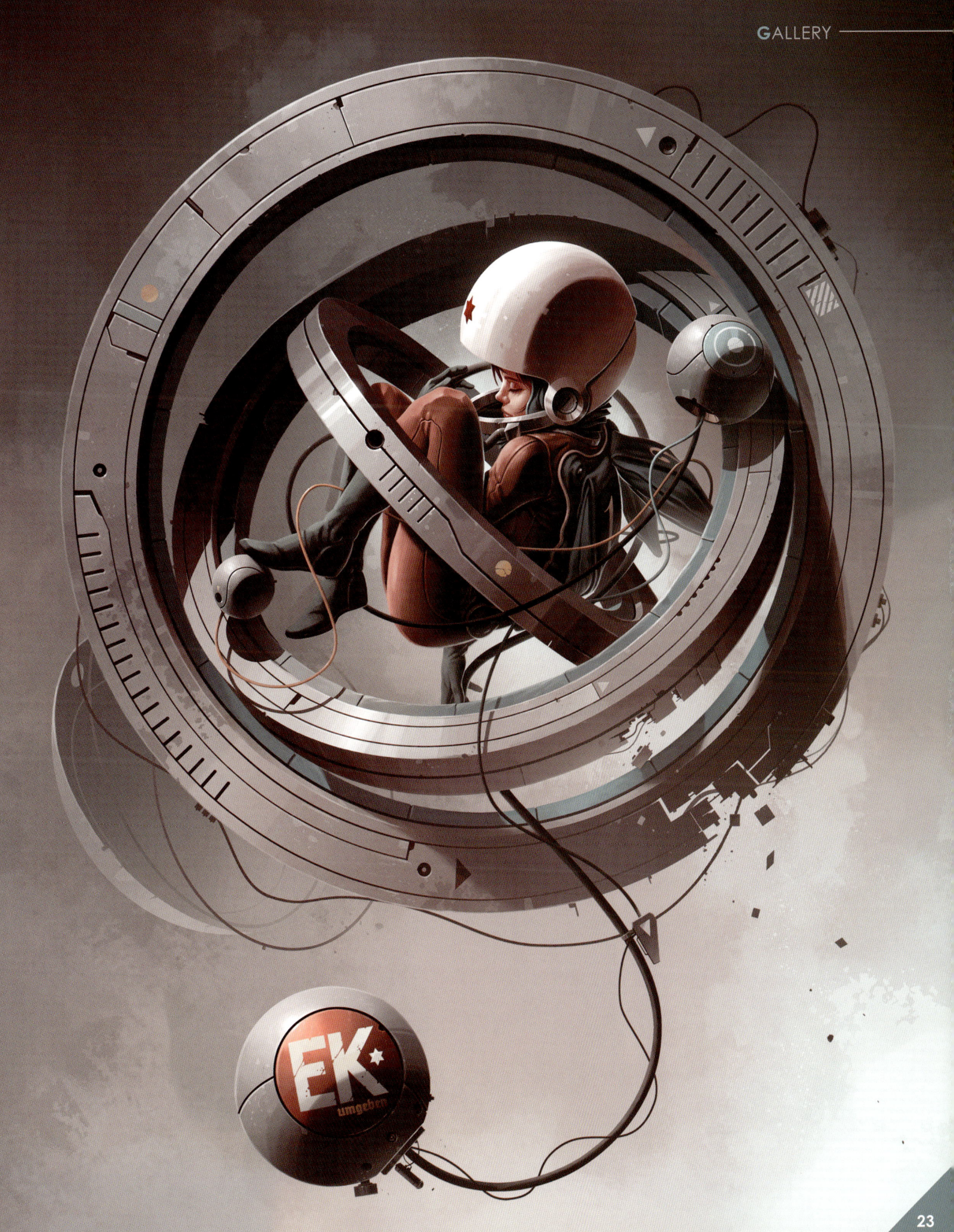

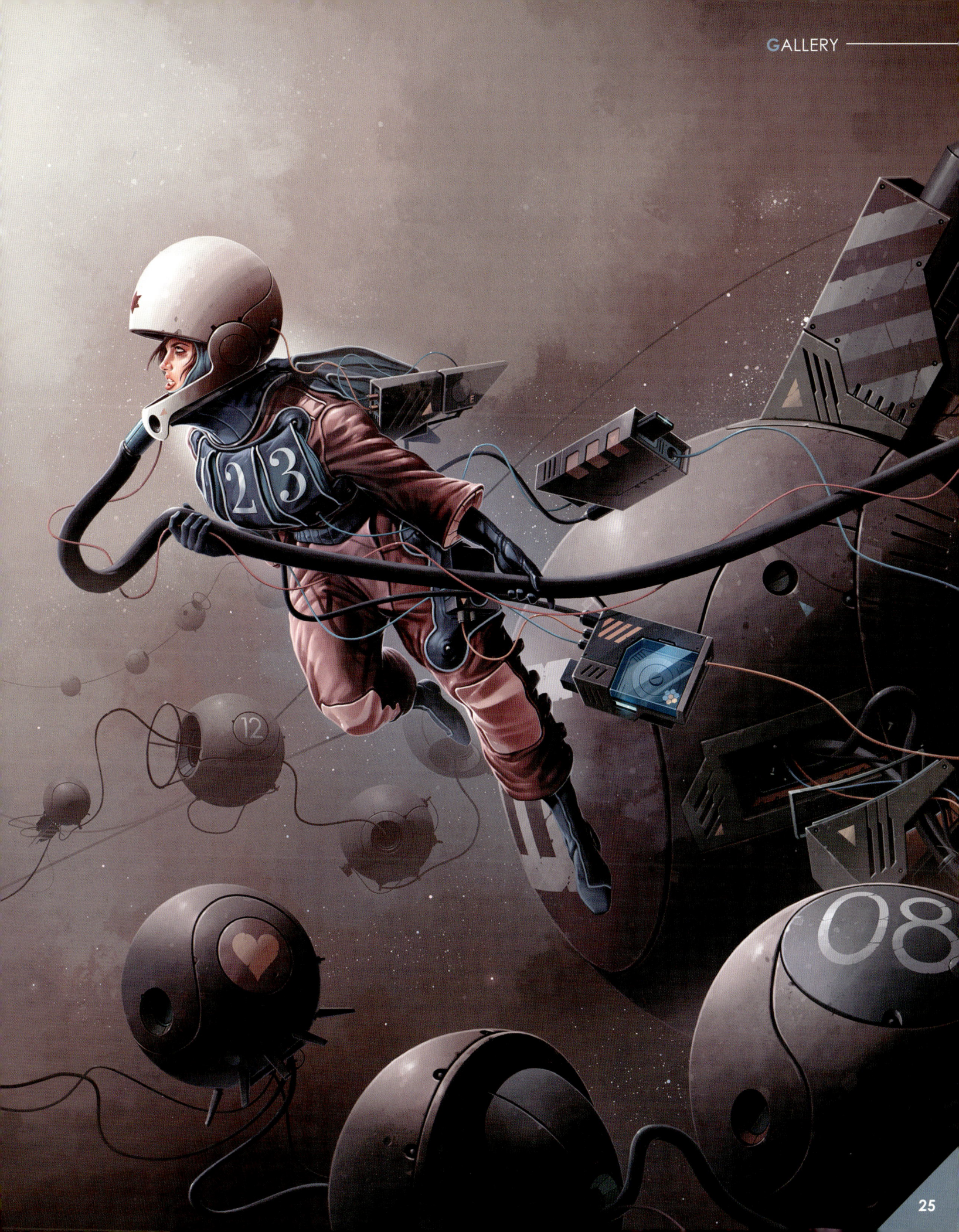

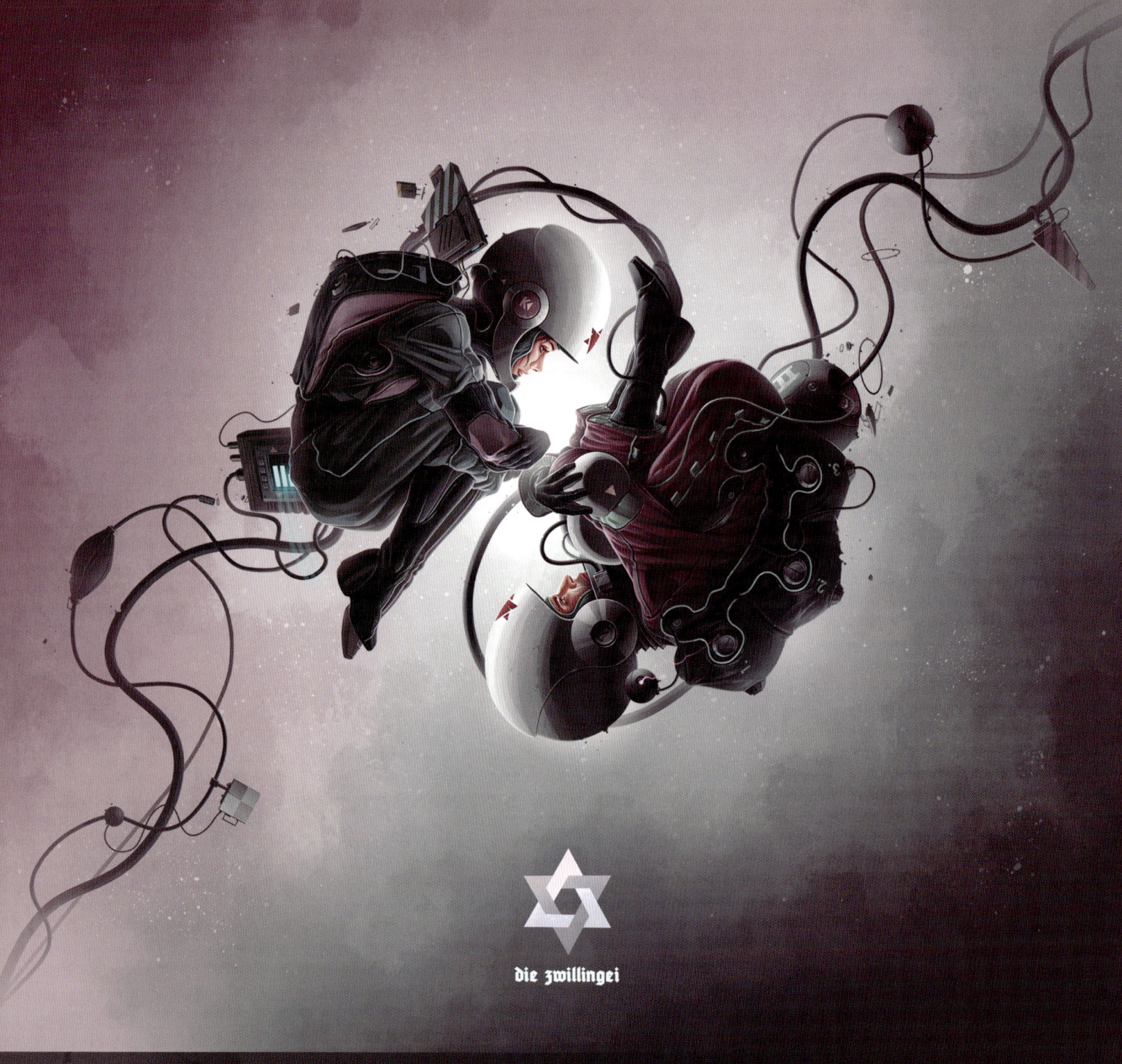

die zwillingei

THE JOURNEY ◄◄ p.24/25
2015, 35"x 23"
2D/3D Digital

This one was a personal commission done for a client to help dress up his new office space and is meant to represent the life journey that he is on with his partner.
I really liked how this one turned out.

THE TWINS ▲
2017, 11"x 8.5"
2D Digital

Another personal commission created for a client out in Toronto, Ontario, Canada. This is perhaps one of the most unique EK pieces for the single fact that it was created to hang in the nursery for the client's baby twins!

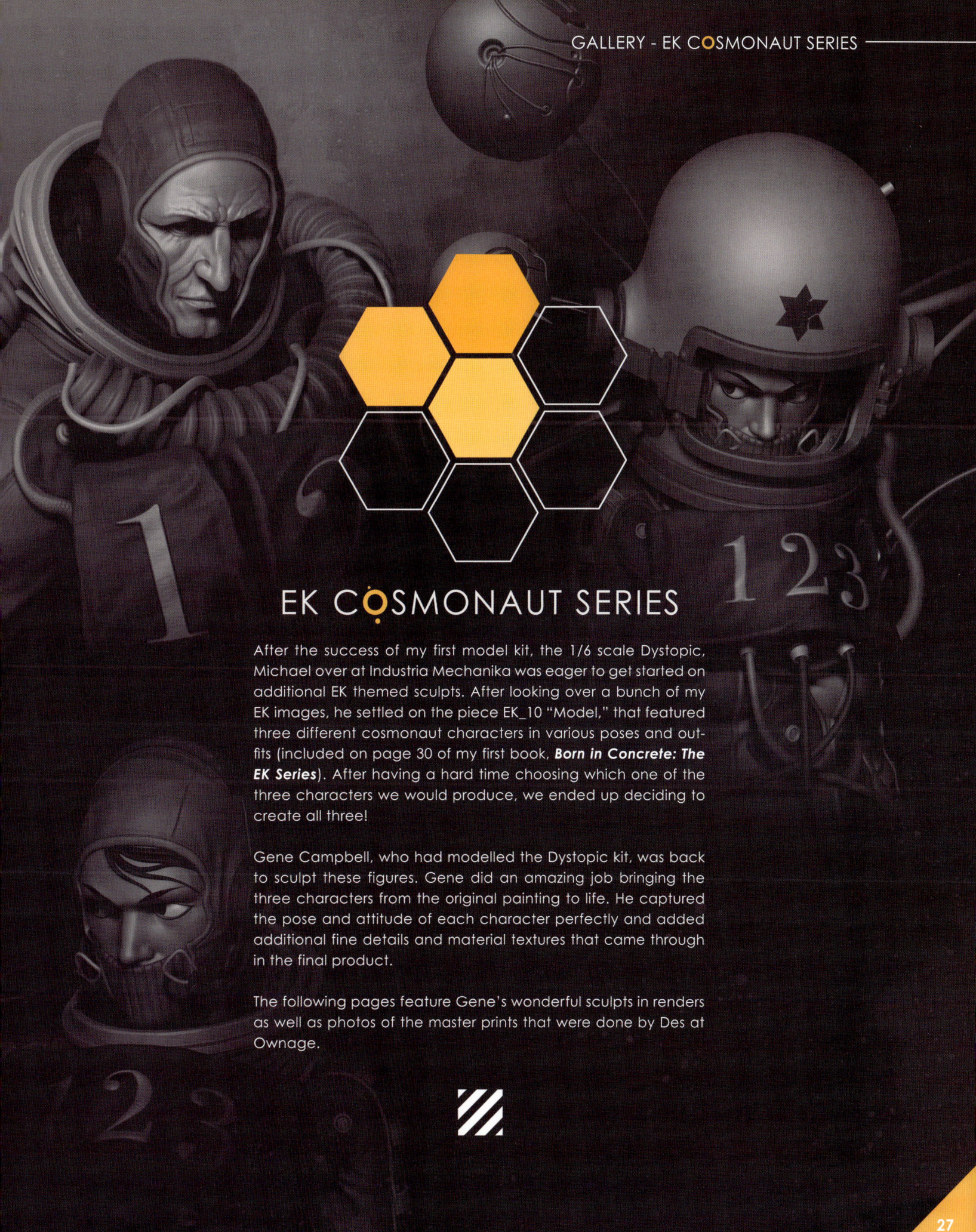

EK COSMONAUT SERIES

After the success of my first model kit, the 1/6 scale Dystopic, Michael over at Industria Mechanika was eager to get started on additional EK themed sculpts. After looking over a bunch of my EK images, he settled on the piece EK_10 "Model," that featured three different cosmonaut characters in various poses and outfits (included on page 30 of my first book, **Born in Concrete: The EK Series**). After having a hard time choosing which one of the three characters we would produce, we ended up deciding to create all three!

Gene Campbell, who had modelled the Dystopic kit, was back to sculpt these figures. Gene did an amazing job bringing the three characters from the original painting to life. He captured the pose and attitude of each character perfectly and added additional fine details and material textures that came through in the final product.

The following pages feature Gene's wonderful sculpts in renders as well as photos of the master prints that were done by Des at Ownage.

EK

COSMONAUT SERIES: FIGURE NO.1

CREATED BY DEREK STENNING
SCULPTED BY GENE CAMPBELL

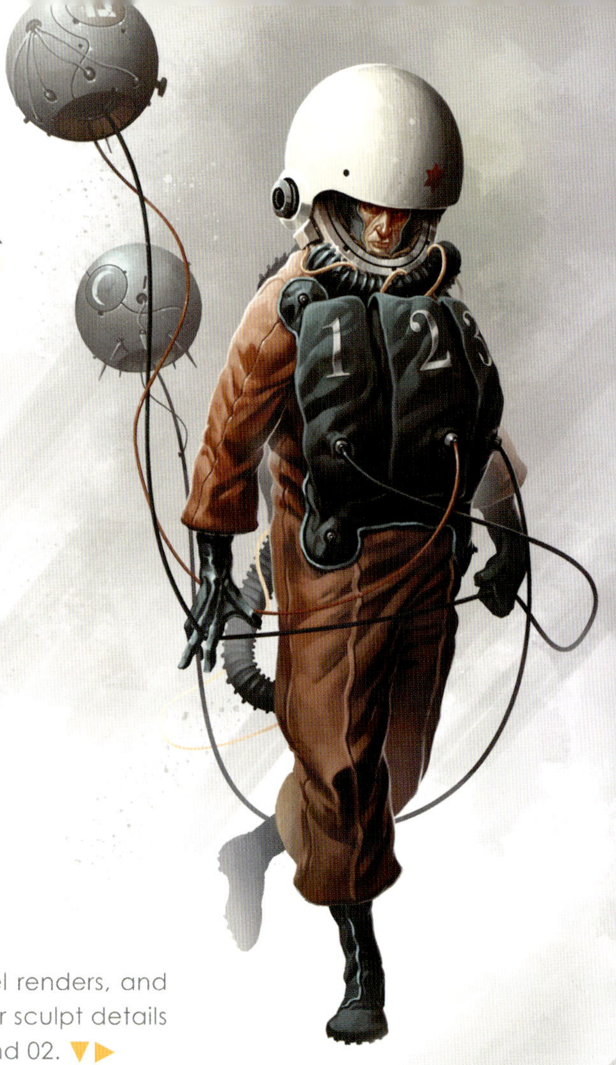

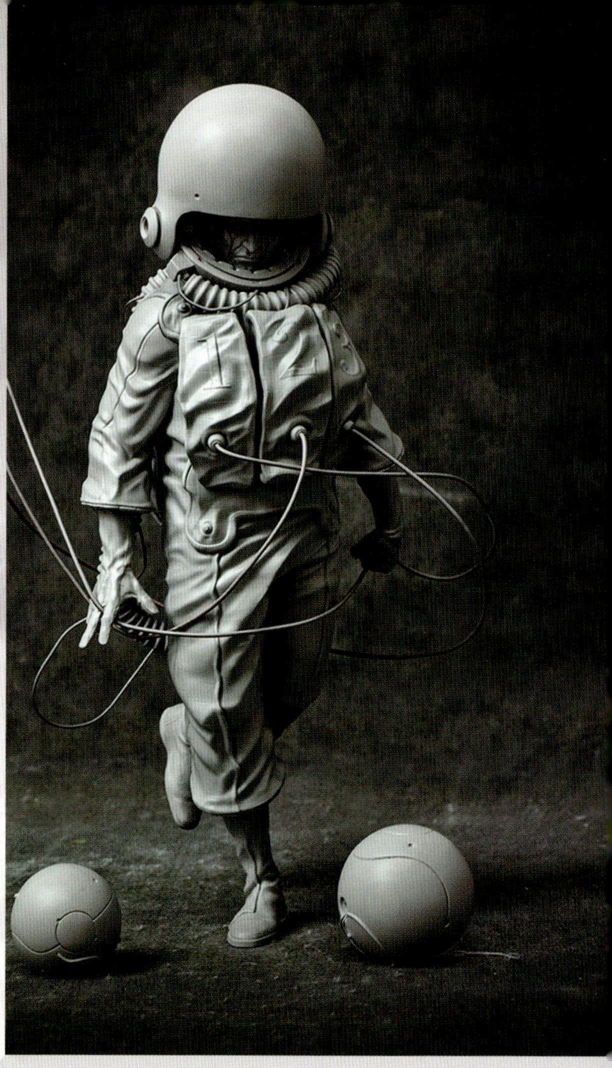

Box art, final model renders, and printed resin master sculpt details for model kits 01 and 02. ▼▶

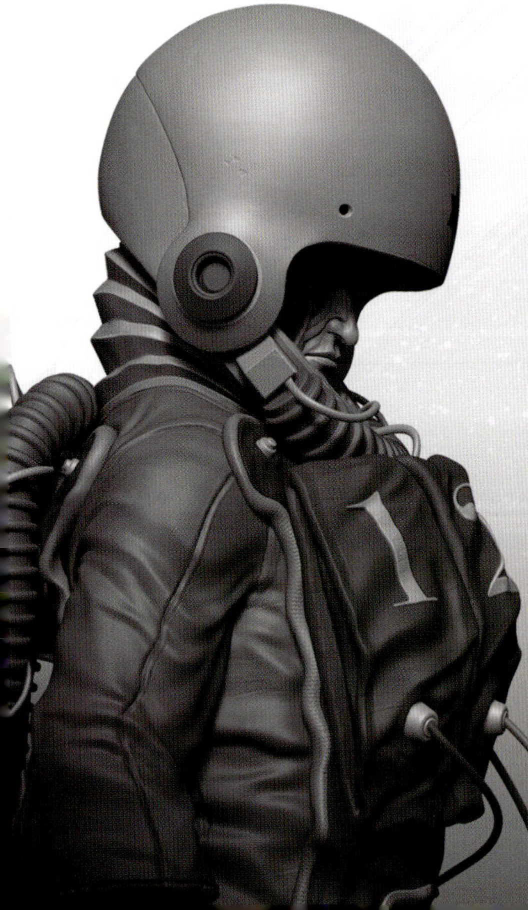

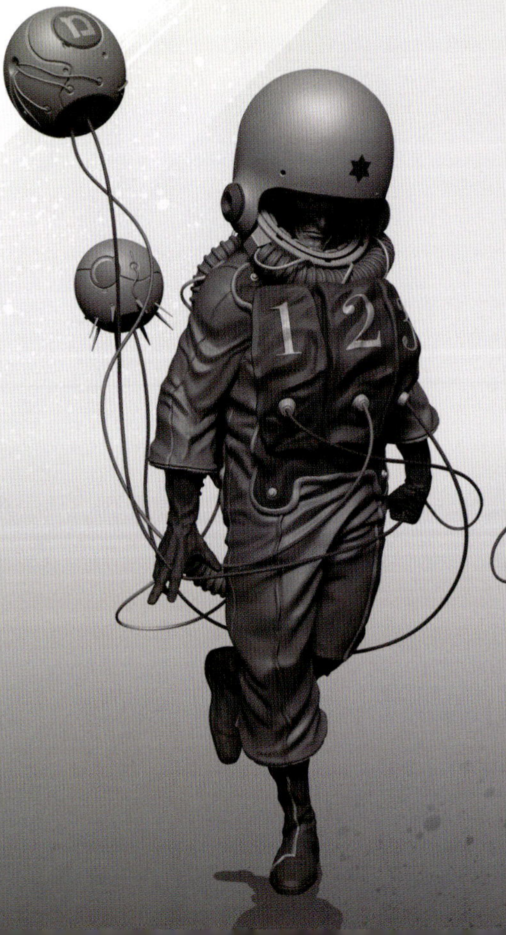

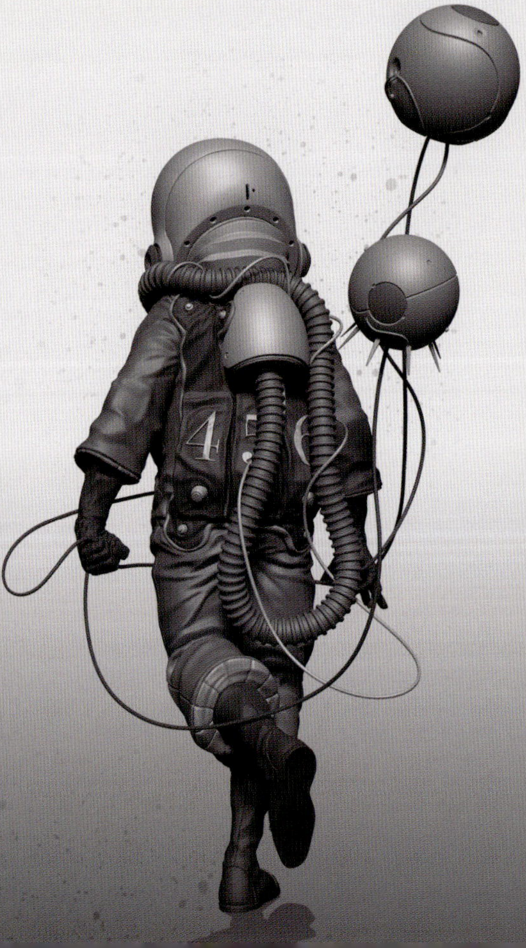

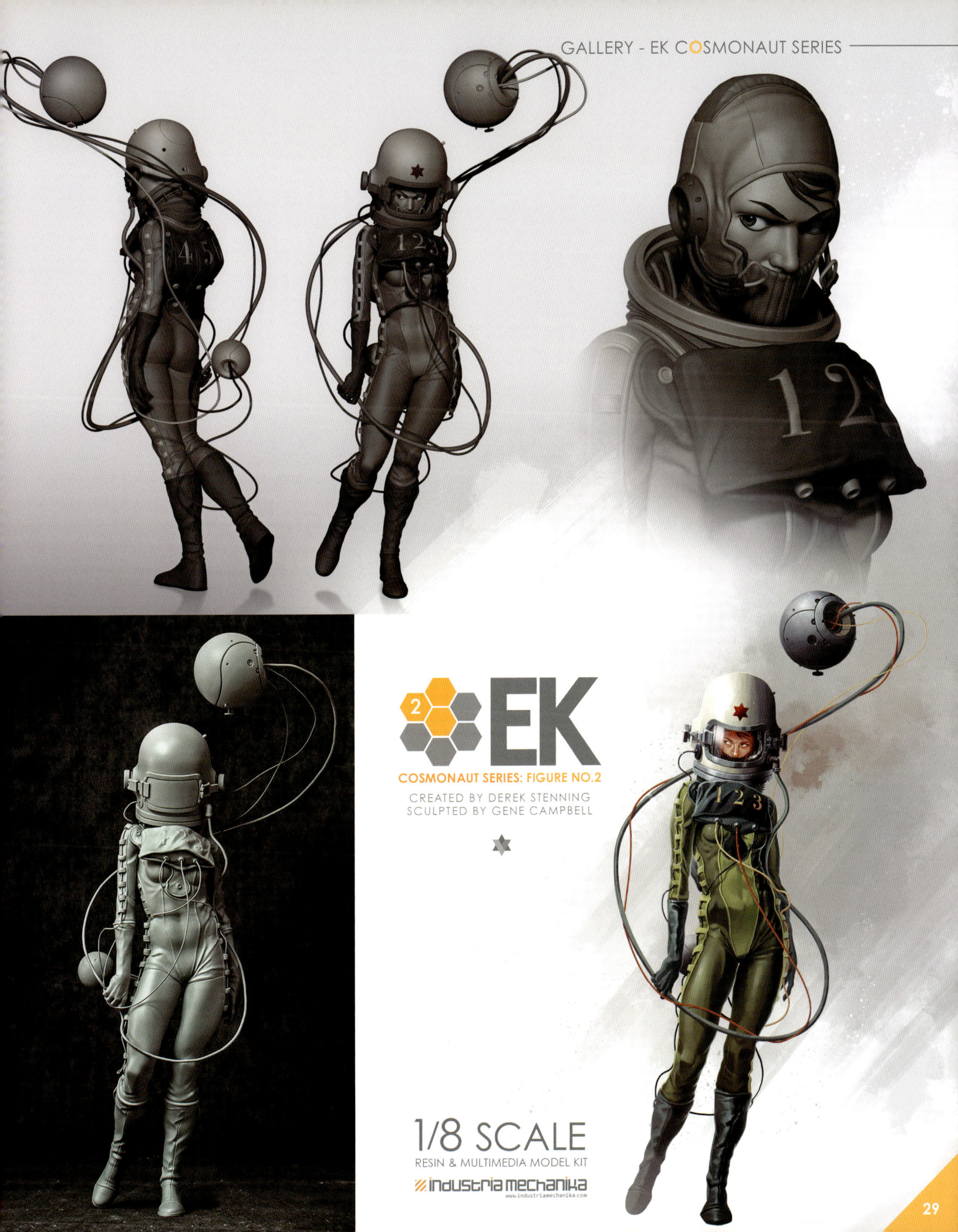

EK

COSMONAUT SERIES: FIGURE NO.2

CREATED BY DEREK STENNING
SCULPTED BY GENE CAMPBELL

1/8 SCALE

RESIN & MULTIMEDIA MODEL KIT

industria mechanika
www.industriamechanika.com

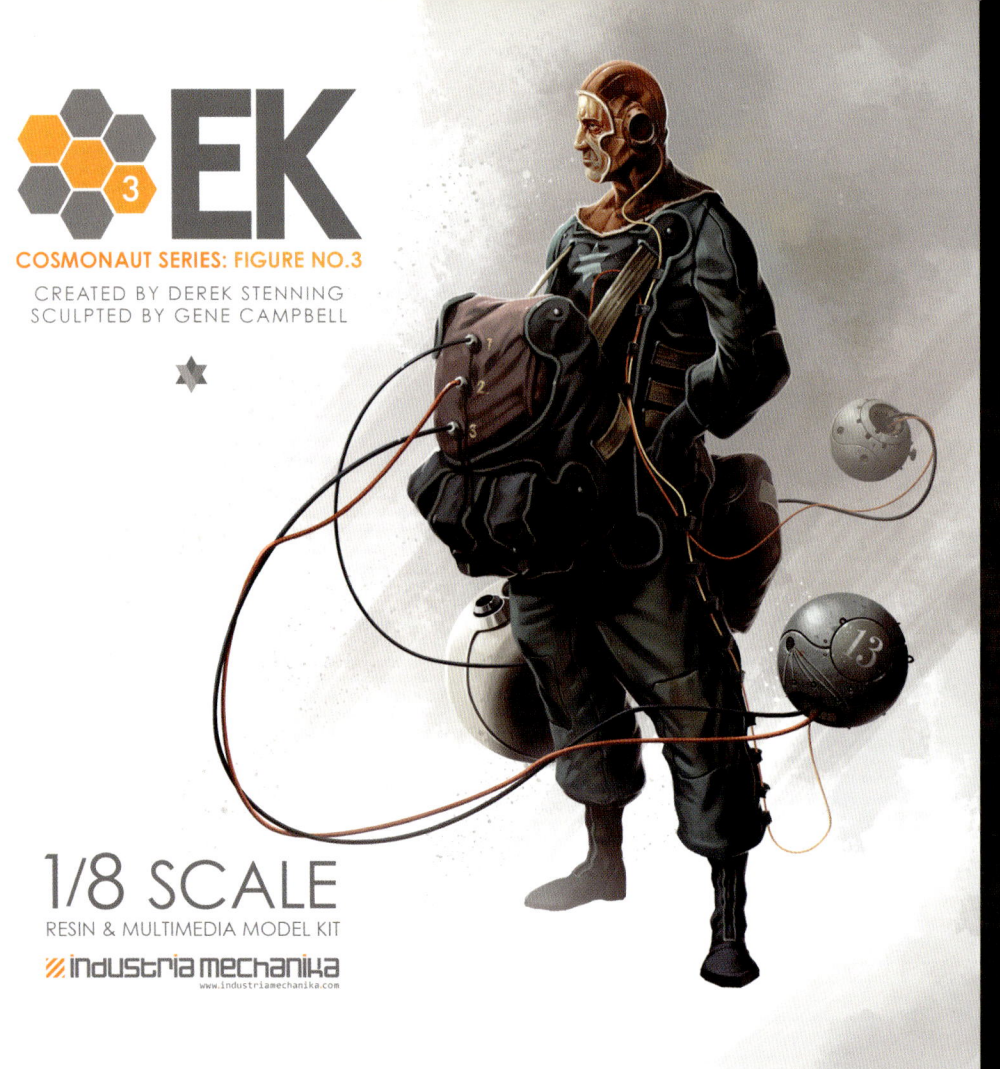
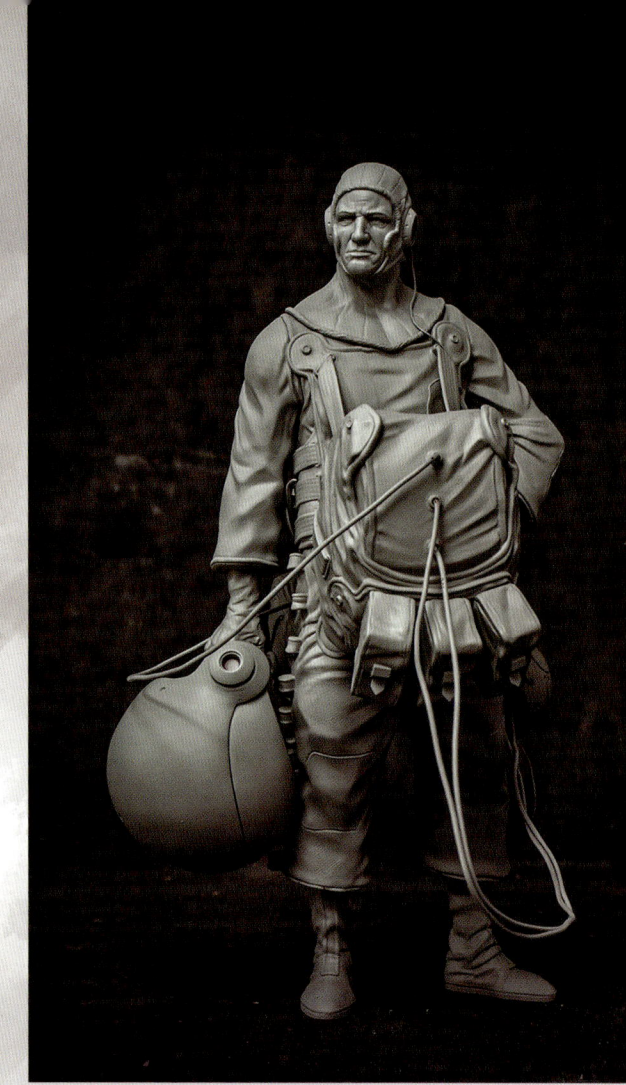

EK

3

COSMONAUT SERIES: FIGURE NO.3

CREATED BY DEREK STENNING
SCULPTED BY GENE CAMPBELL

1/8 SCALE
RESIN & MULTIMEDIA MODEL KIT

industria mechanika
www.industriamechanika.com

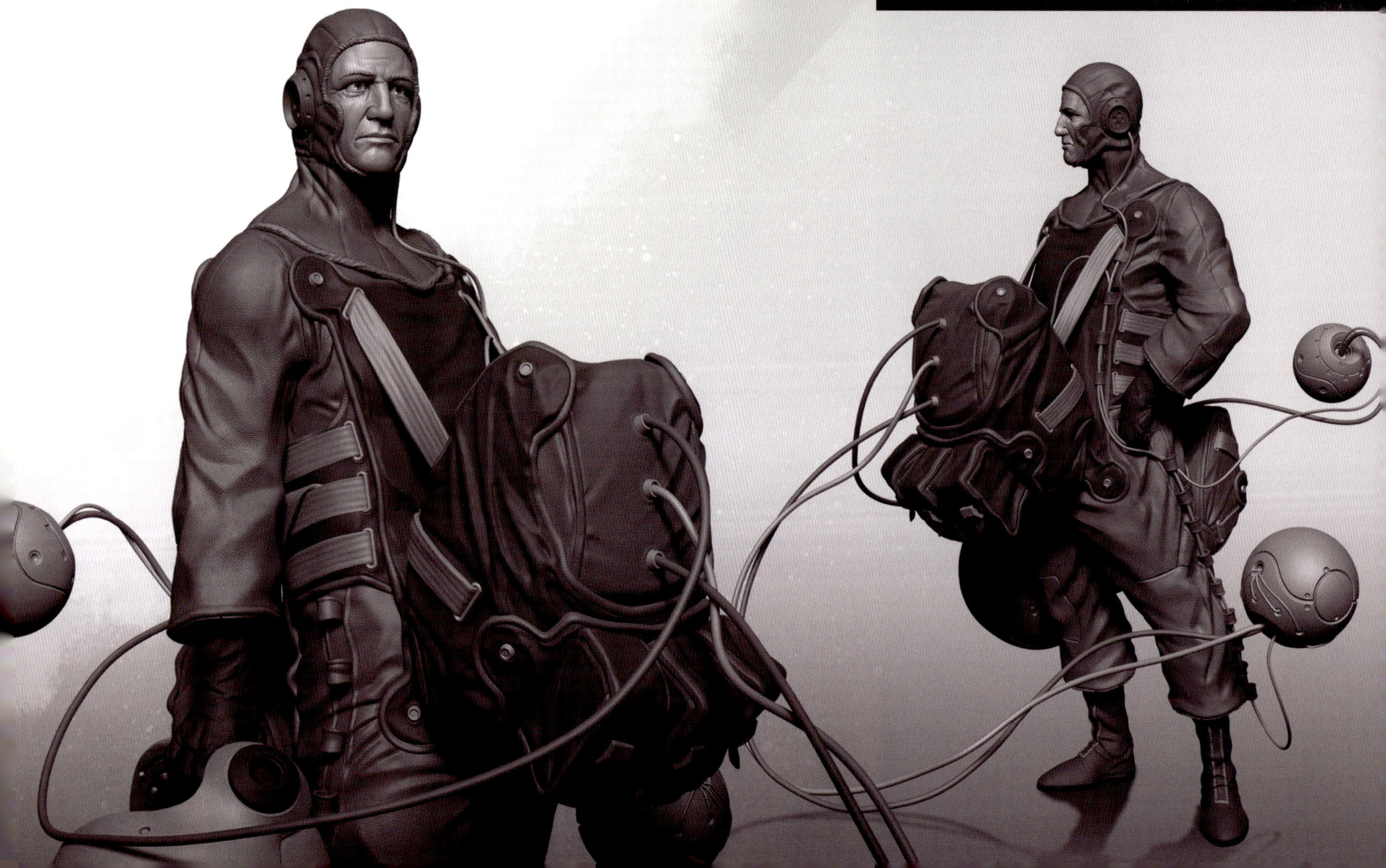

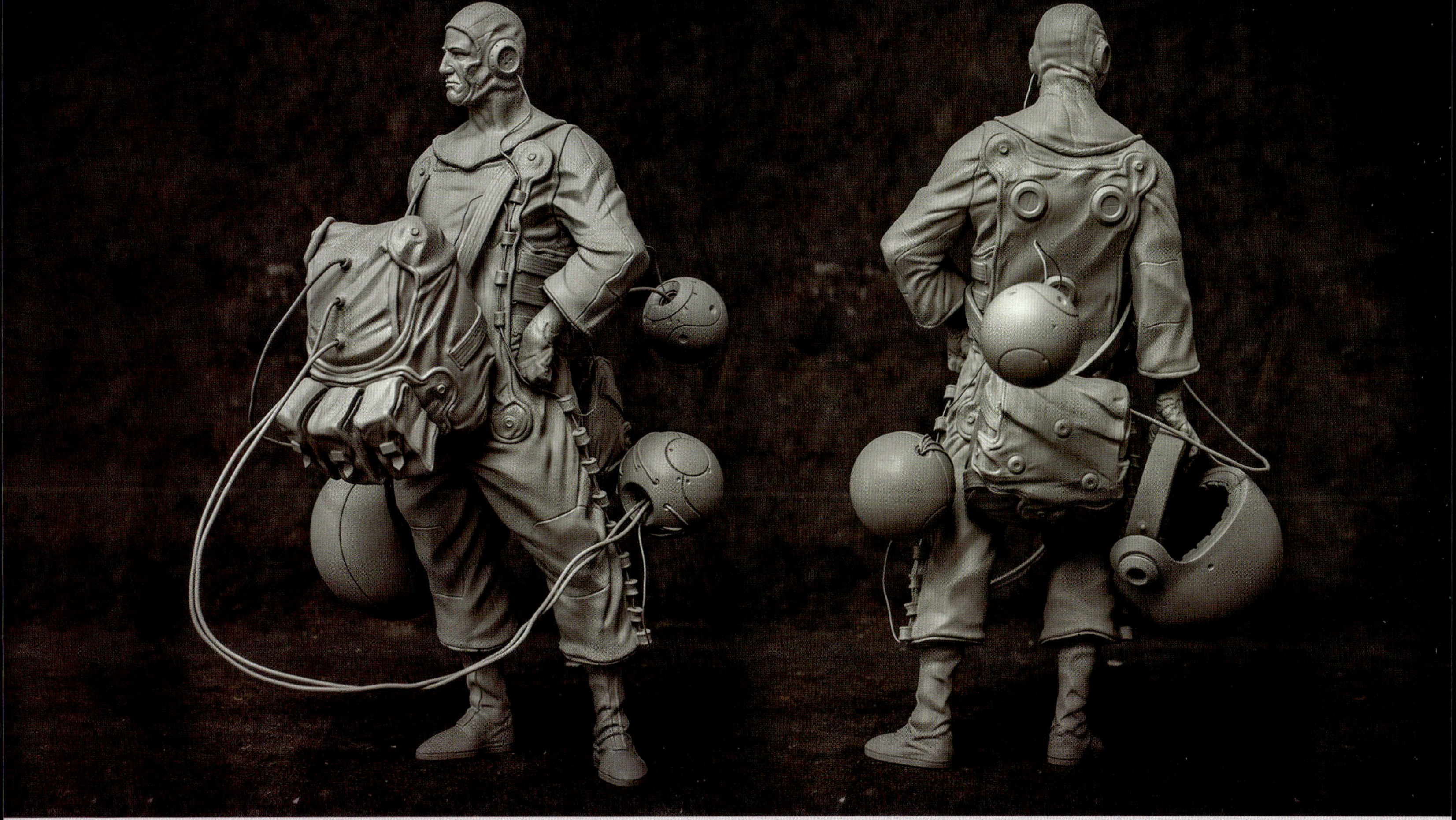

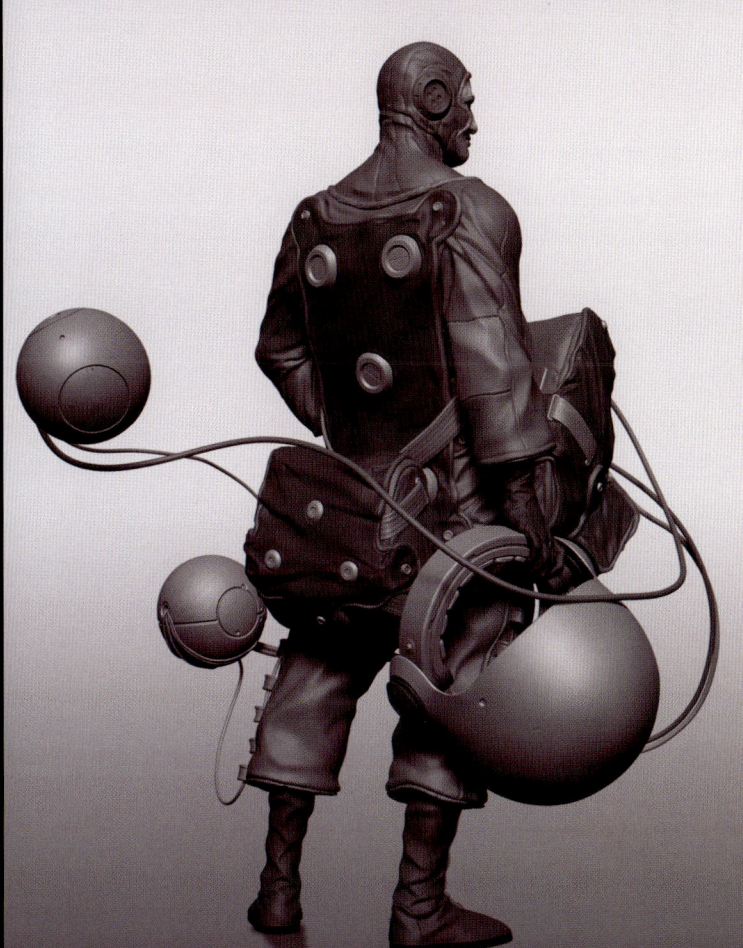

Box art, model renders and printed master sculpt details for EK Cosmonaut Kit 03. ◀▲

These three kits, labelled EK Cosmonaut #01, #02, and #03 were first released one per year from 2014 to 2016. Somehow, we ended up releasing them in reverse order, starting with #03 and ending with #01. I don't know why.

The kits proved to be popular, with kits #02 and #03 selling especially well, and all three kits remained in production up to summer of 2021, when Industria Mechanika ceased producing physical resin model kits.

These kits were also important in that, apart from a few prints available on my website, these were the only "new" EK pieces to see the light of day during those years.

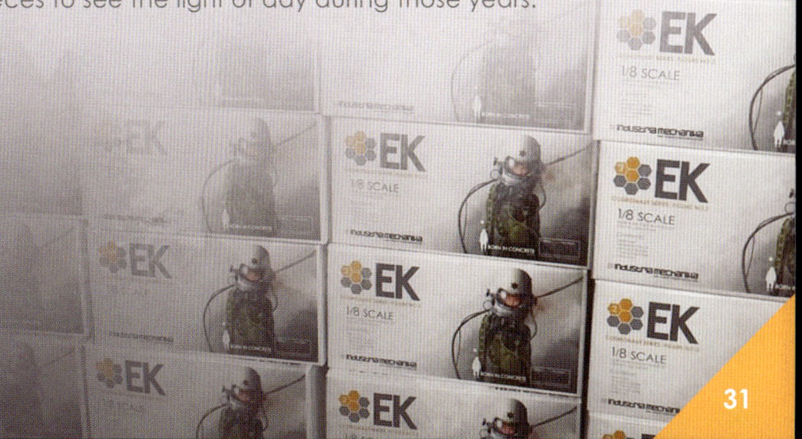

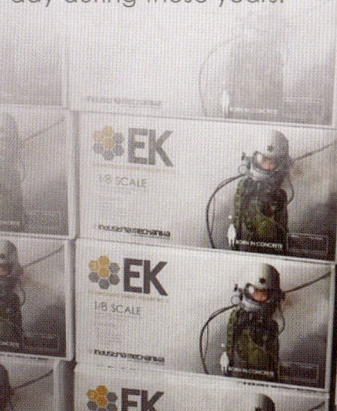

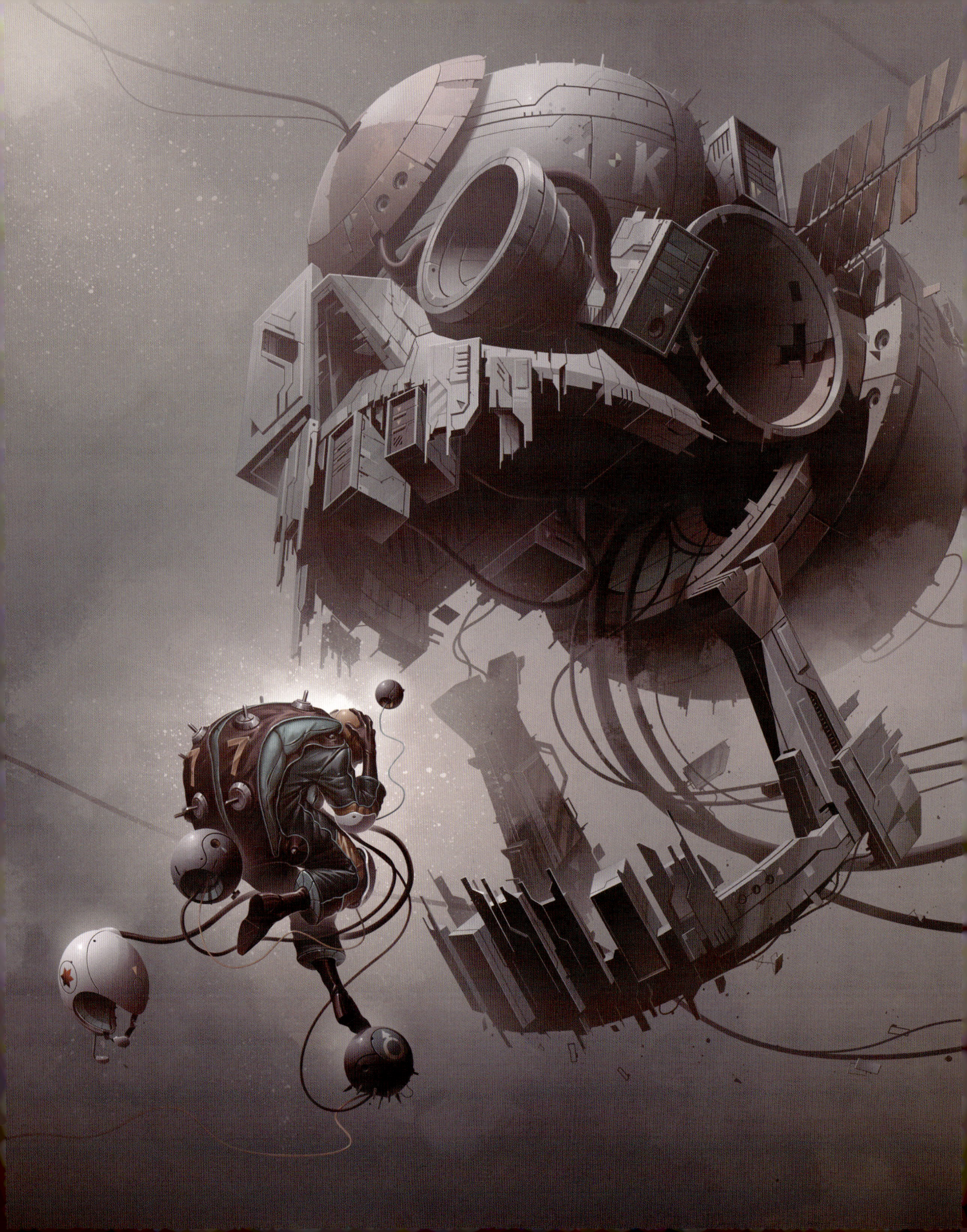

UNHOLINESS ARRIVES BY SATELLITE

UNHOLINESS ARRIVES BY SATELLITE
2017, 28"x 16"
Graphite, 2D/3D Digital

This one is about someone close to you, someone in your orbit, who is devouring you.

As mentioned, soon after we returned home from living in Europe, my father was diagnosed with vascular dementia. As his cognitive abilities quickly declined, he required more and more assistance in his daily life. As his condition progressed, he pushed away all of his friends and family members and only wanted me to help him with his needs. This left me in the position as his primary caregiver, and this situation began to swallow up more and more of my life.

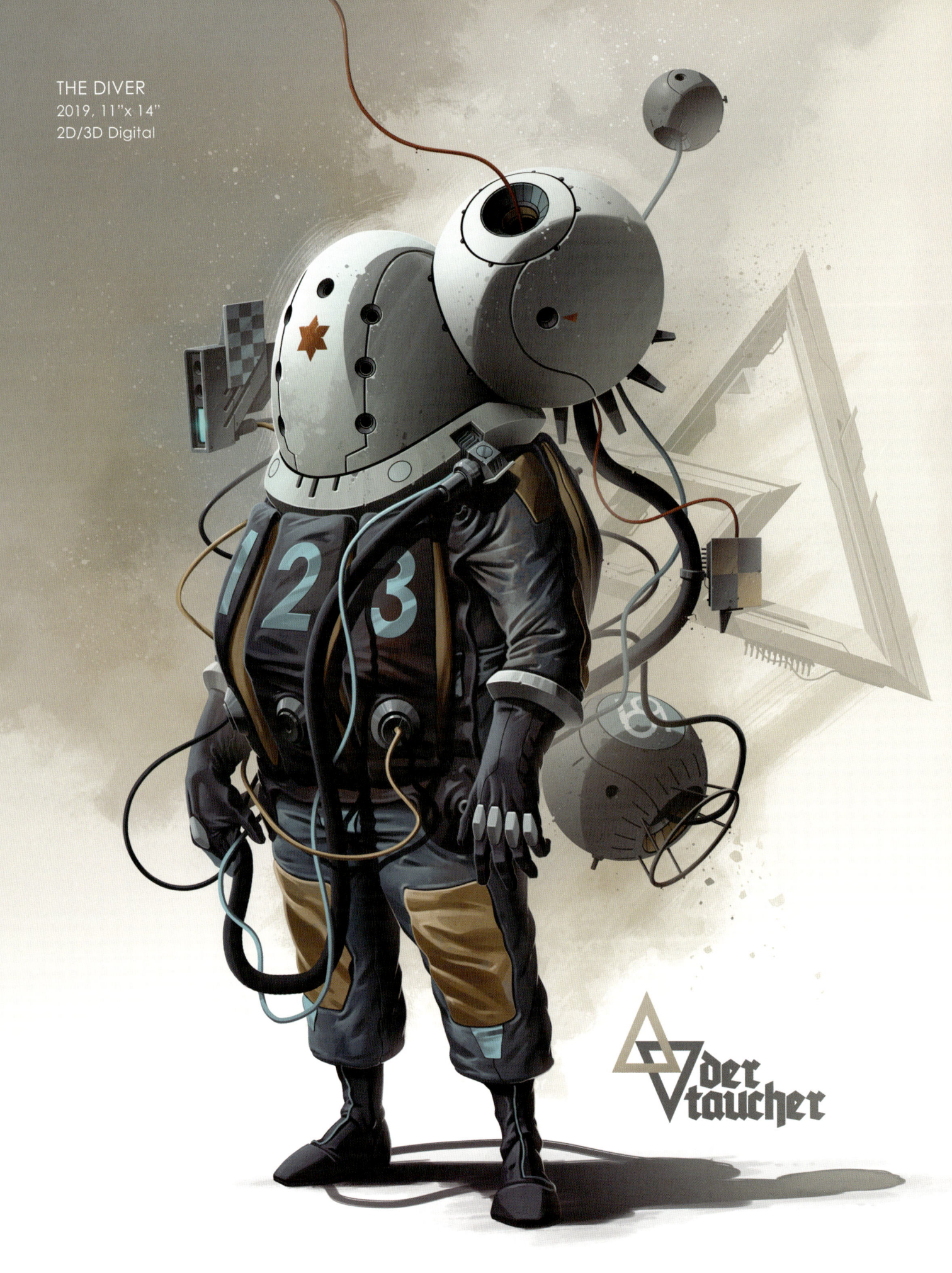

THE DIVER
2019, 11"x 14"
2D/3D Digital

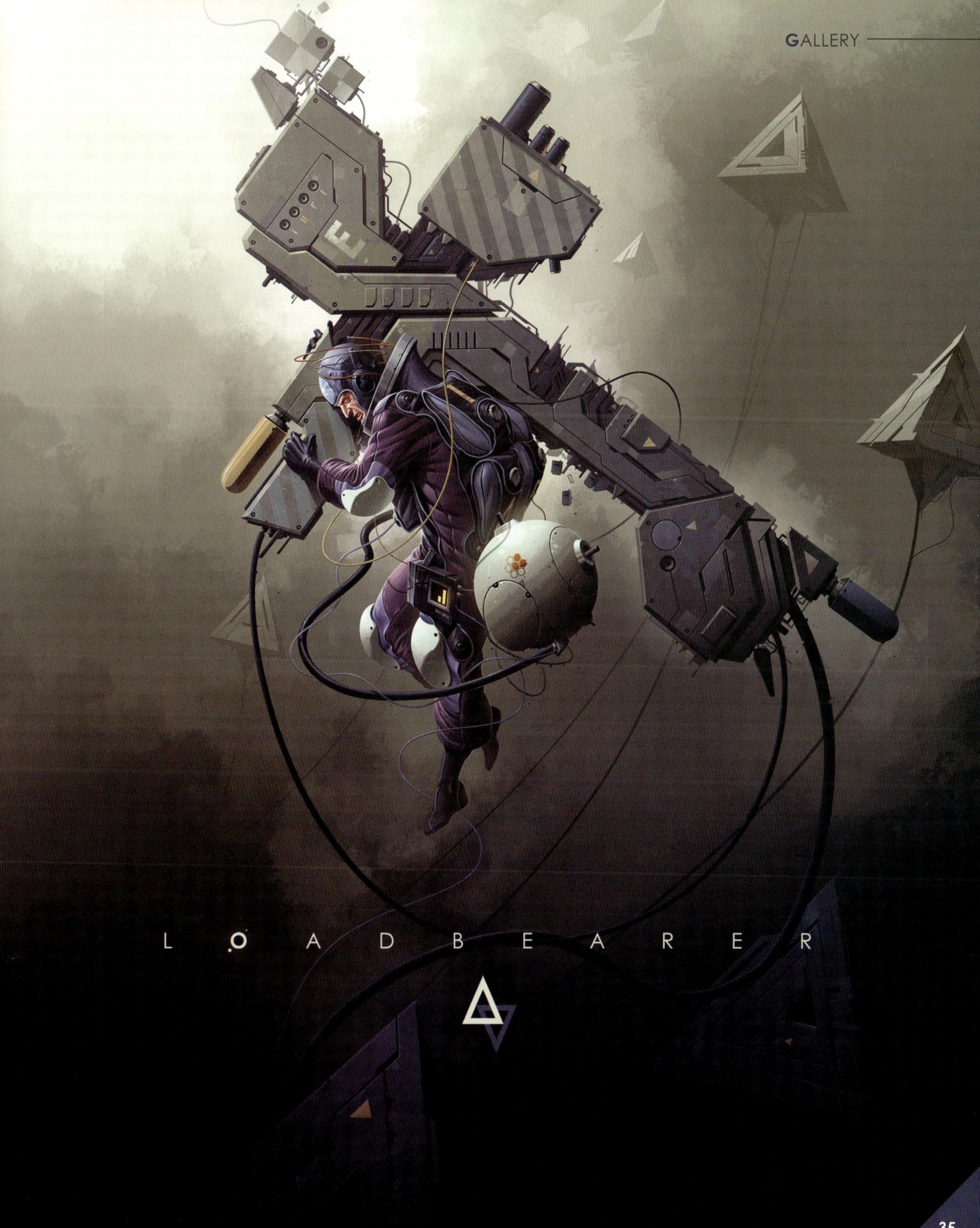

LOADBEARER

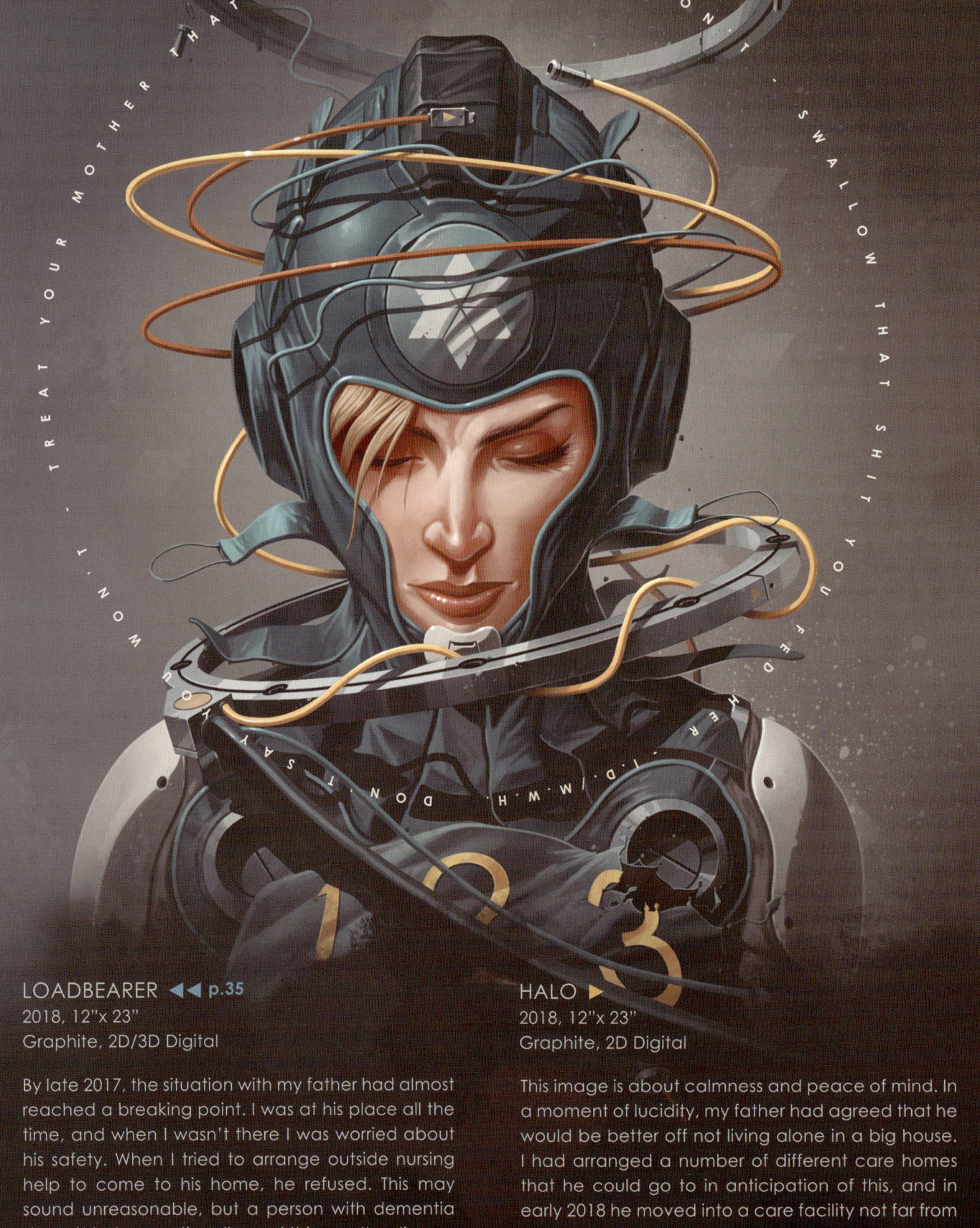

TREAT YOUR MOTHER THAT · WON'T · TREAT YOUR MOTHER THAT

WON'T · SWALLOW THAT SHIT YOU FED HER · I'D W.H.M.W · DON'T SAY YOU

LOADBEARER ◀◀ p.35
2018, 12"x 23"
Graphite, 2D/3D Digital

By late 2017, the situation with my father had almost
reached a breaking point. I was at his place all the
time, and when I wasn't there I was worried about
his safety. When I tried to arrange outside nursing
help to come to his home, he refused. This may
sound unreasonable, but a person with dementia
doesn't behave rationally, and this was the disease
making these decisions, not the father I knew and
loved. Again, with this commitment added to my
work and family life, I felt like I was loaded down or
carrying a huge weight, and this piece is the result of
this (but I'm unsure of the cross imagery.....)

HALO ▶
2018, 12"x 23"
Graphite, 2D Digital

This image is about calmness and peace of mind. In
a moment of lucidity, my father had agreed that he
would be better off not living alone in a big house.
I had arranged a number of different care homes
that he could go to in anticipation of this, and in
early 2018 he moved into a care facility not far from
my house. On the day he moved in, I had the best
sleep I had had in months. Halo is the first piece I did
for myself after I regained some sense of balance in
my life. It is meant to speak to the peace and the
relief that I felt now that my father was getting more

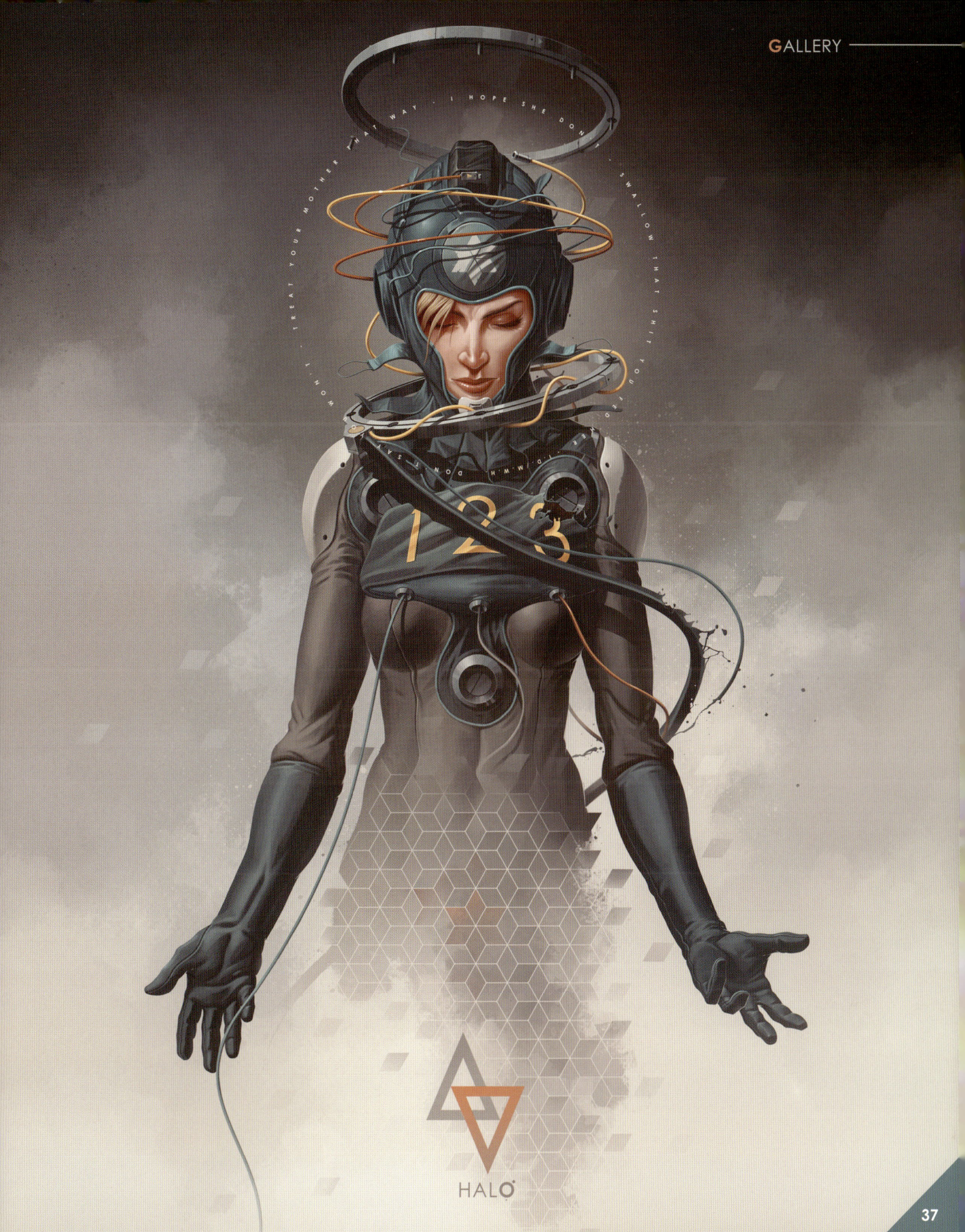

HALO

DUCHESS

1/6 SCALE RESIN MODEL KIT

By the time the last figure in the EK Cosmonaut Series was released, Michael and I began to talk about creating another EK model kit design. My first model kit, the 1/6 scale Dystopic figure was still selling well, and both Michael and I were interested in creating a companion piece of sorts: another 1/6 scale kit that would complement Dystopic. I also wanted to create something that contrasted the original kit, so the large orb was brought up over the figure, and the character would be female and feature a more formfitting outfit. Gene Campbell was brought in again to handle the sculpting of the piece, and as usual, he did a fantastic job. The creation of the kit was a little more complicated, as the large orb suspended over the figure, and just the sheer size of the kit caused various production and balance issues. After several long delays, the first edition of the Duchess kit was made available for preorders in January 2019 and quickly sold out. The first batch shipped in the spring, and a second edition soon followed.

Unfortunately, this was to be the last EK model kit to feature Gene's amazing sculpting talents. Gene is a busy guy, and for various reasons he decided to step away after the completion of this sculpt. He will be missed. He was very good at translating my style into three dimensions, and he always made my work look better than it is. I'm super thankful for his contributions to the EK Series. I definitely owe that guy a beer!

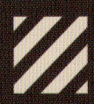

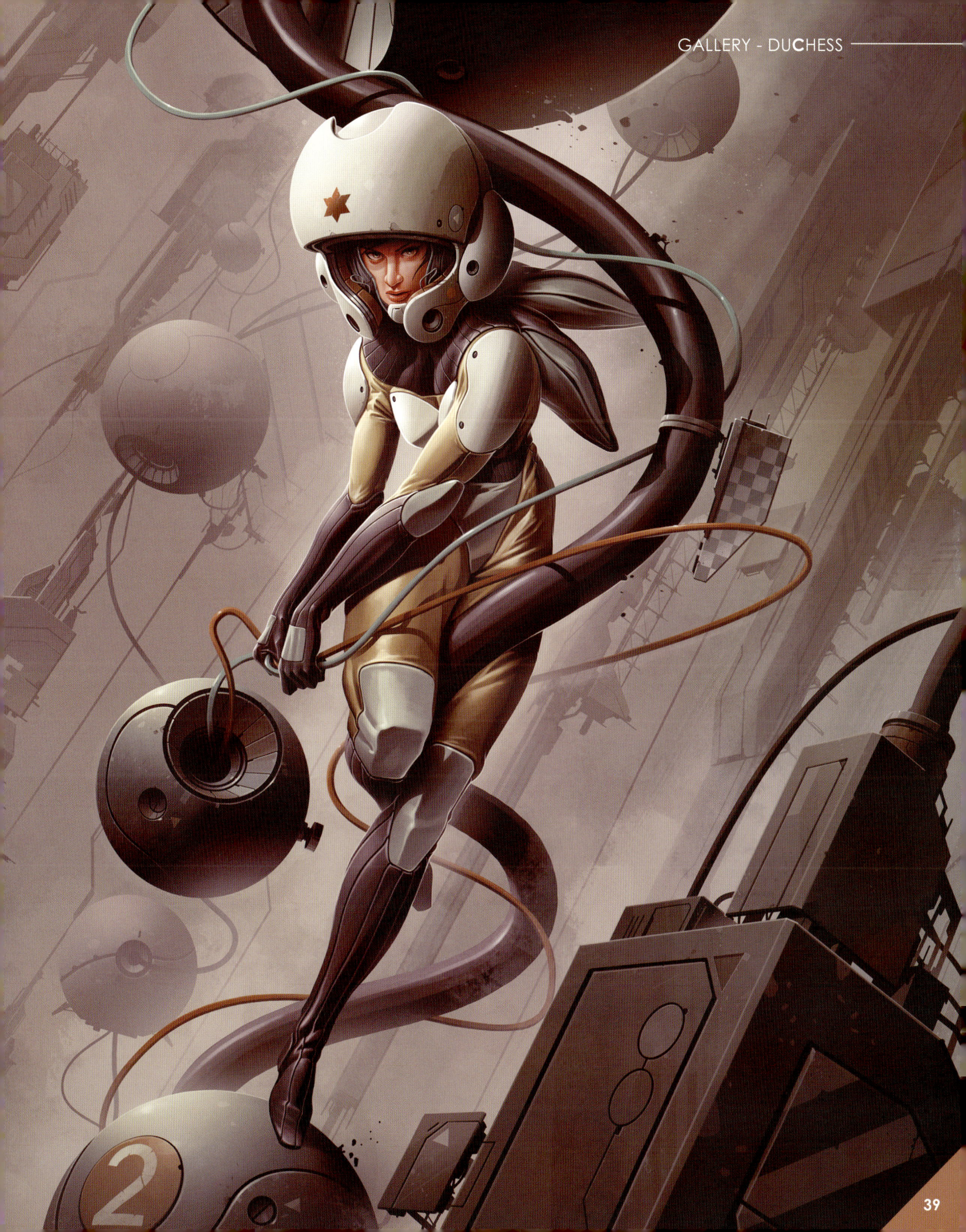

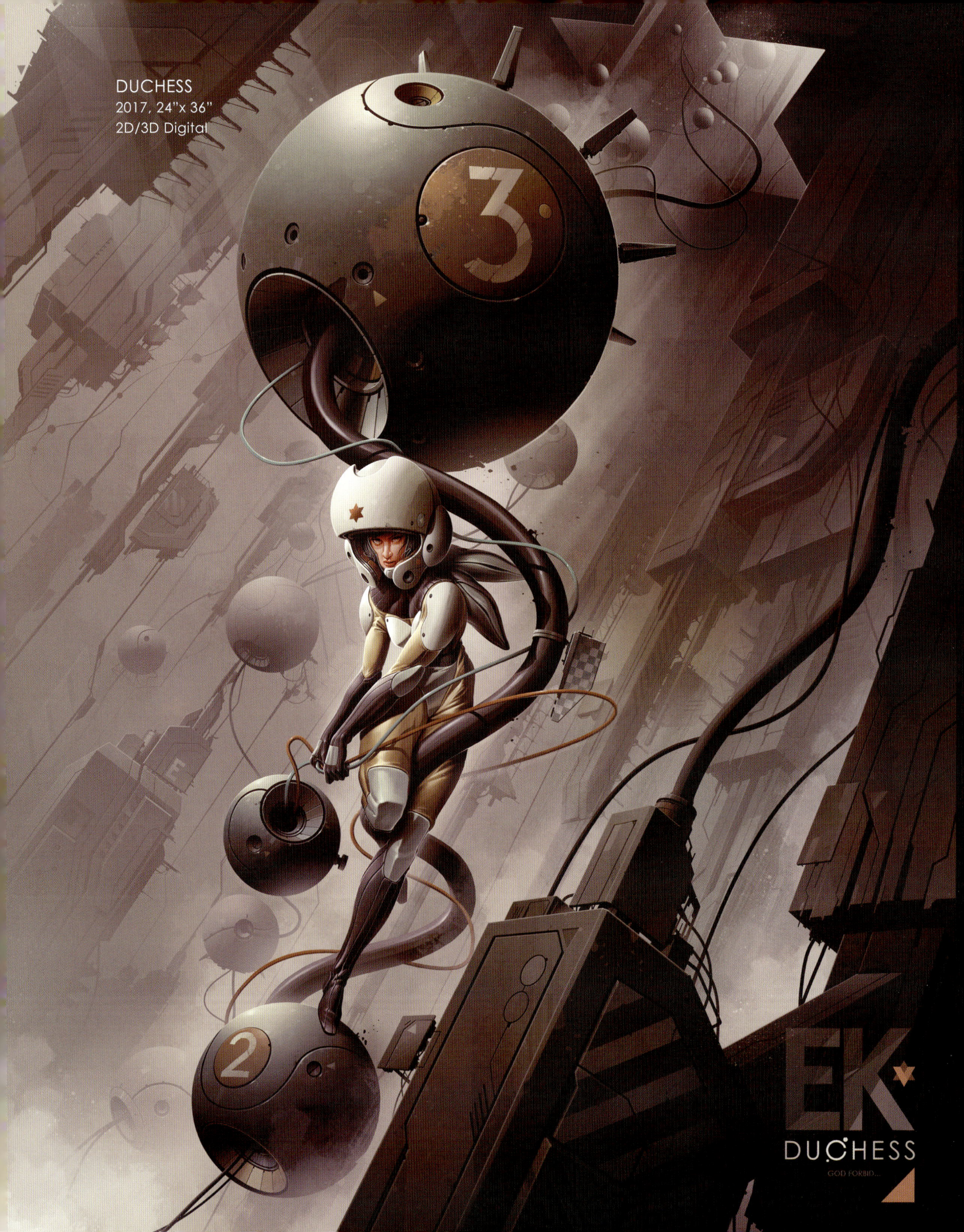

DUCHESS
2017, 24"x 36"
2D/3D Digital

EK

DUCHESS

GOD FORBID...

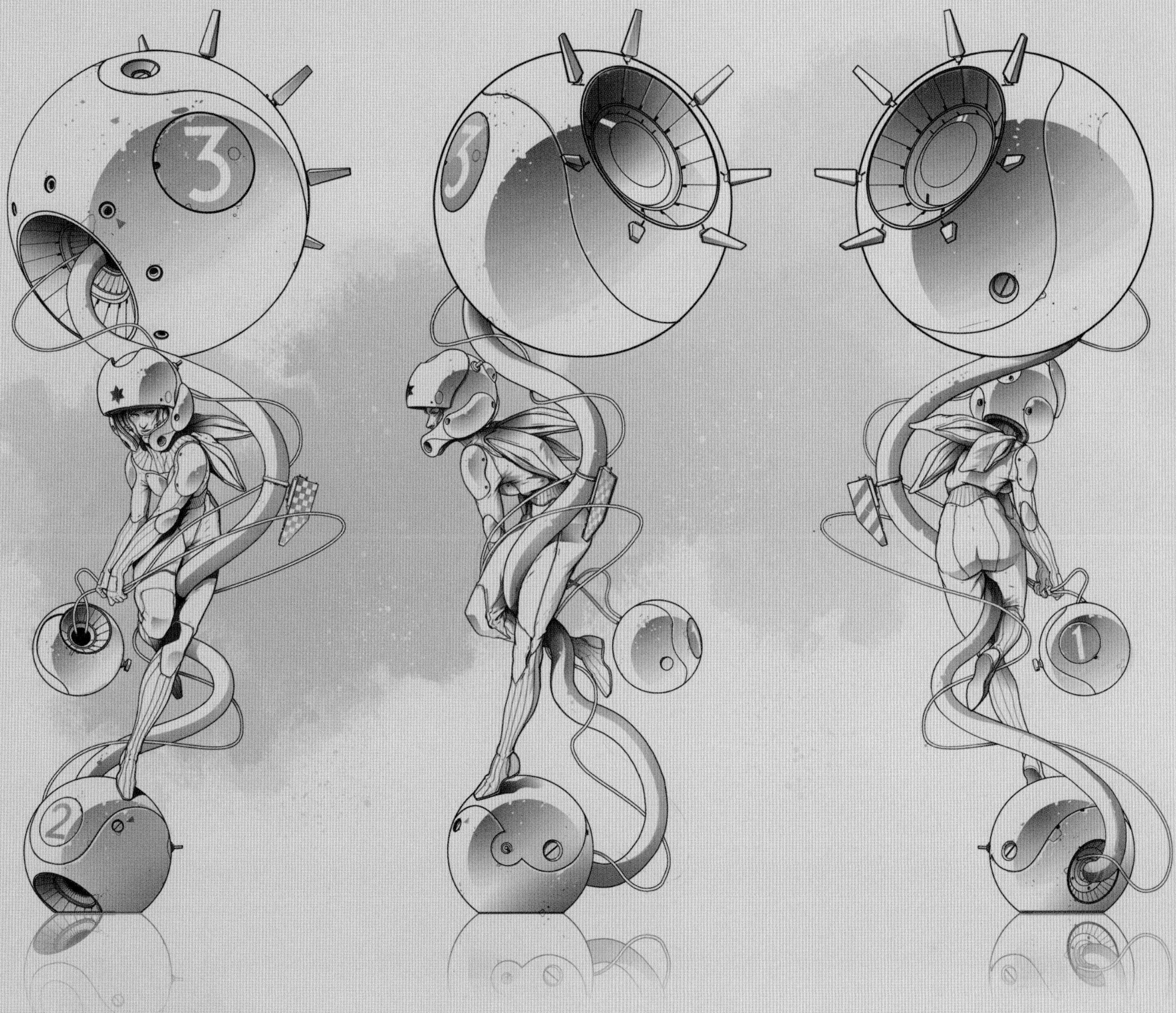

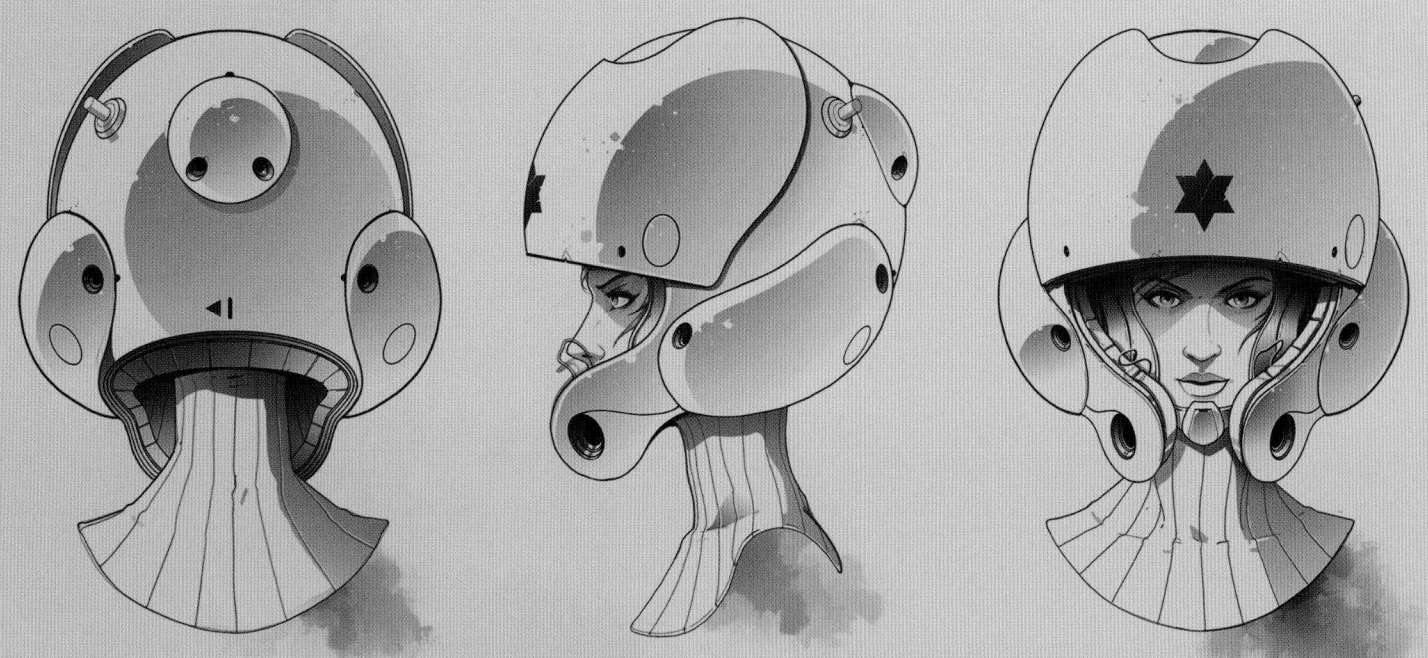

Full body and head/helmet turnaround images created to help inform Gene's 3D sculpt of the figure.

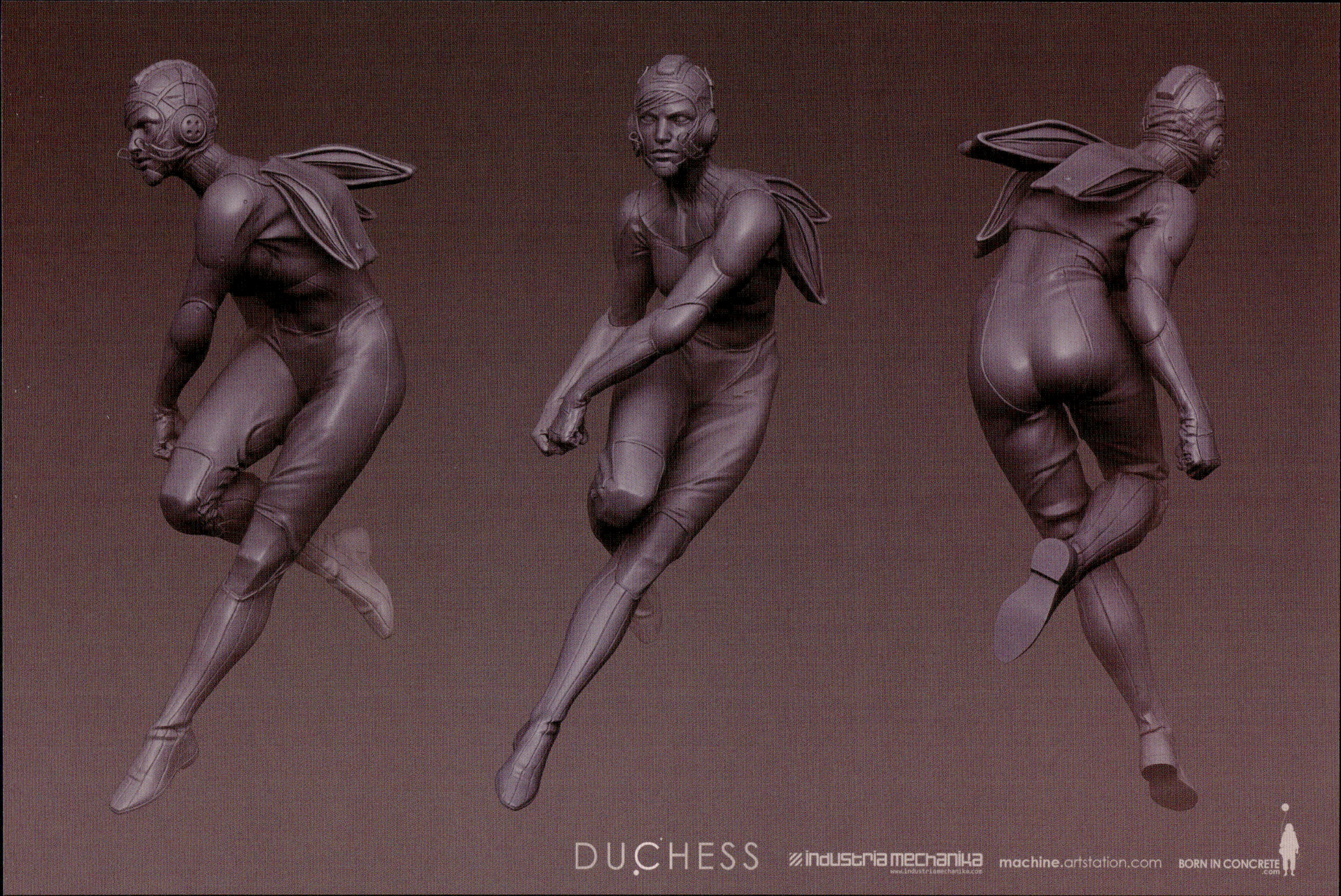

DUCHESS

▲ Renders of the main figure. Gene did a great job capturing the style and movement of the character.

▼ A couple promotional images featuring the final model and highlighting Gene's attention to detail.

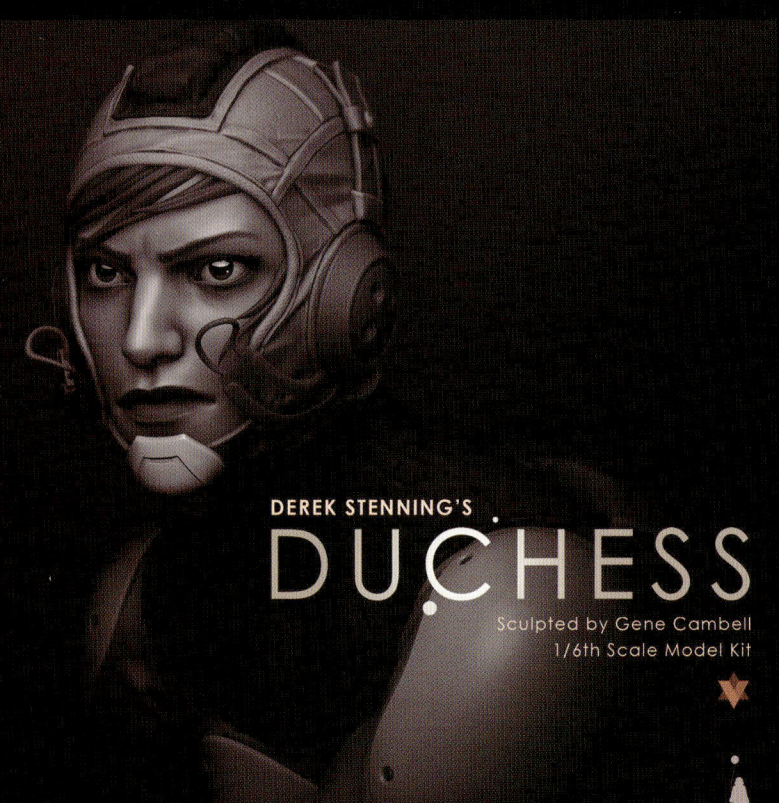

DEREK STENNING'S

DUCHESS

Sculpted by Gene Cambell
1/6th Scale Model Kit

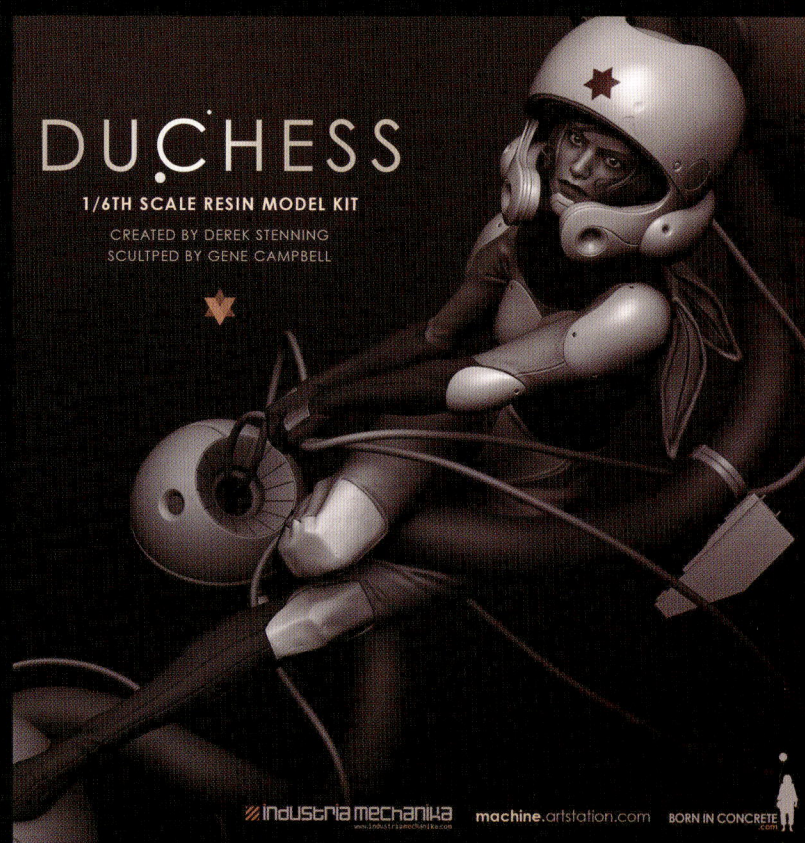

DUCHESS

1/6TH SCALE RESIN MODEL KIT

CREATED BY DEREK STENNING
SCULPTED BY GENE CAMPBELL

Turnaround of the final model, with all the orbs and cables added.

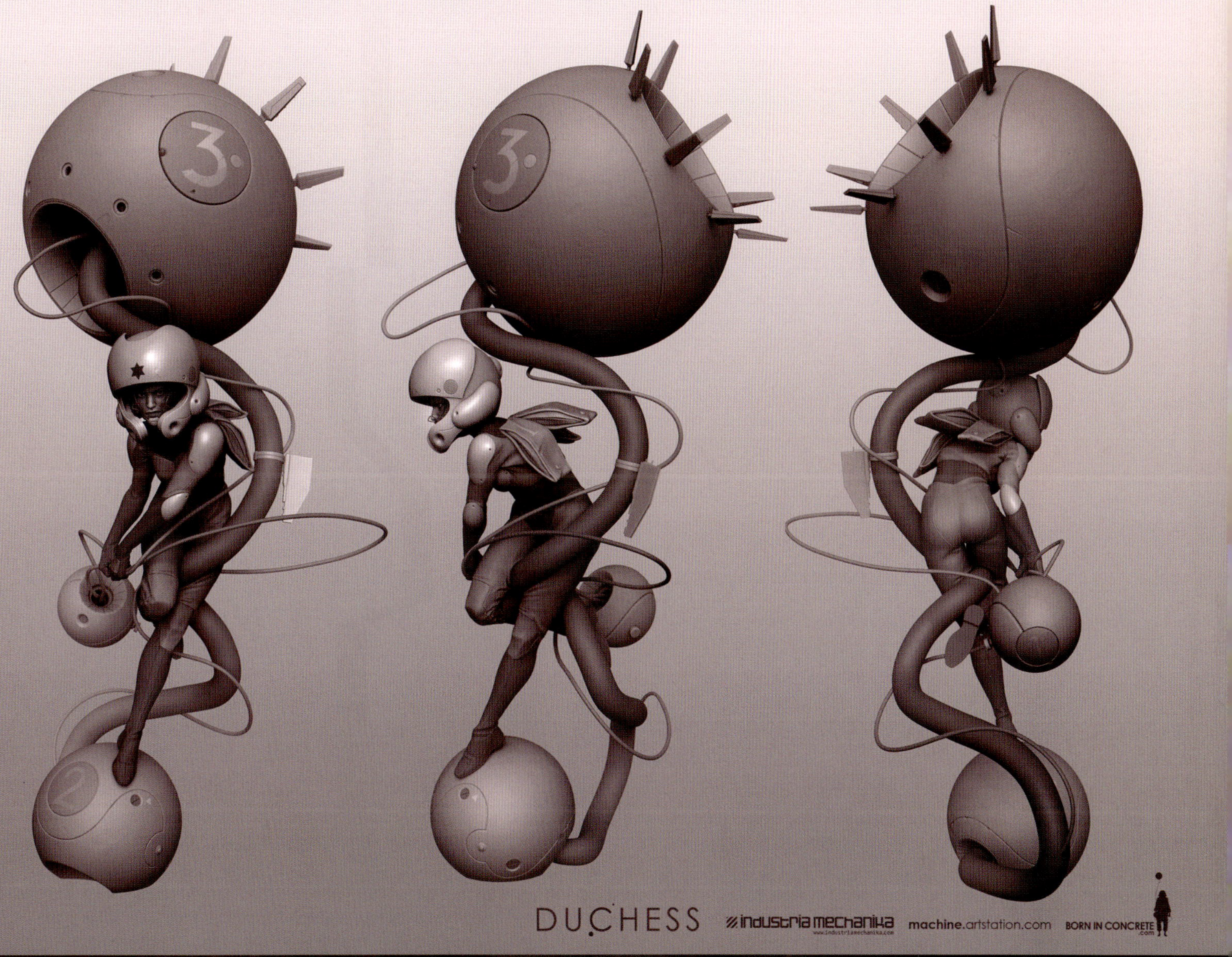

DUCHESS ⫸industria mechanika machine.artstation.com BORN IN CONCRETE.com
www.industriamechanika.com

The final master sculpt elements, printed by Des at Ownage, that were used to create the molds for the cast resin parts of the model kits.

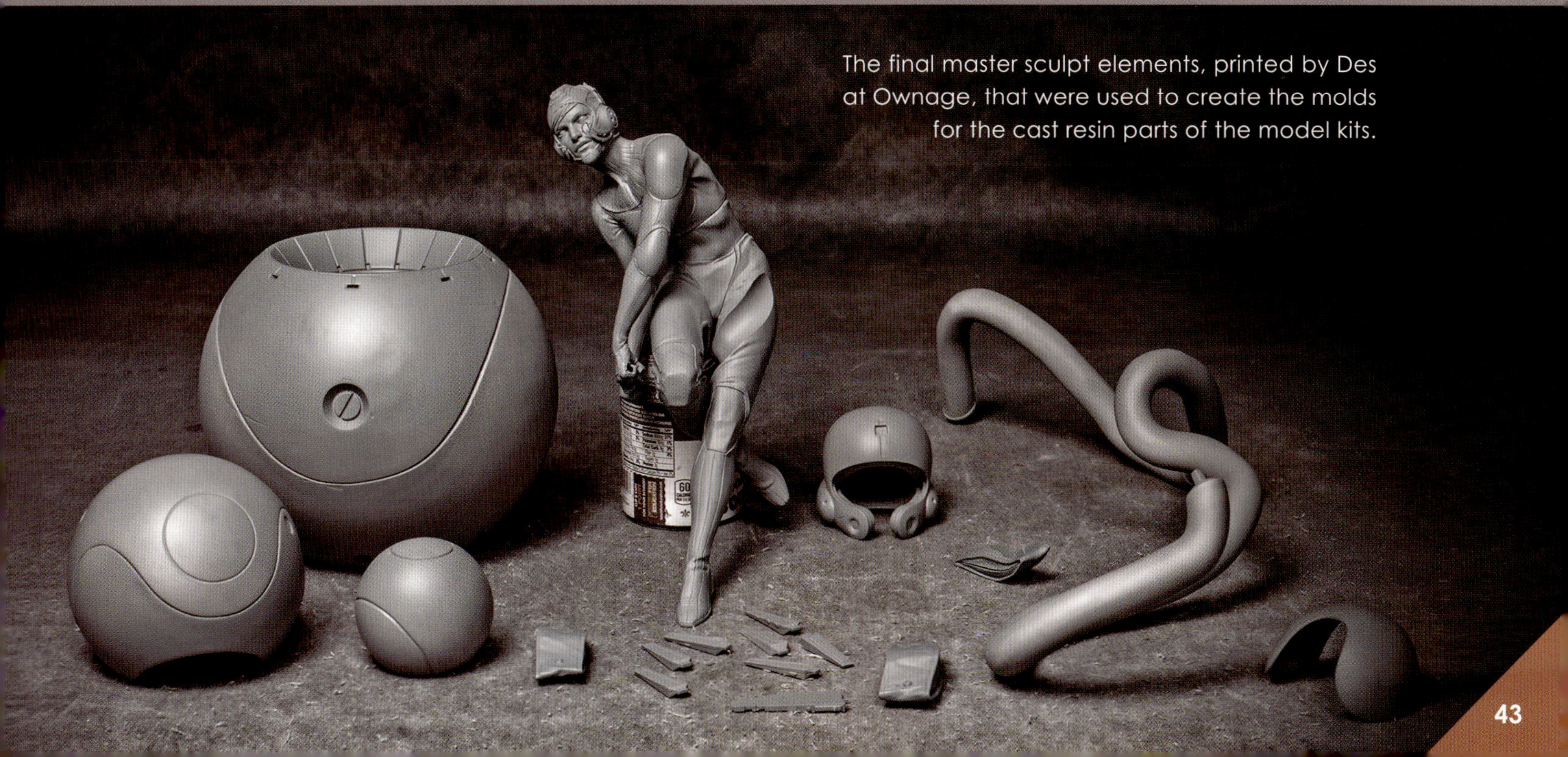

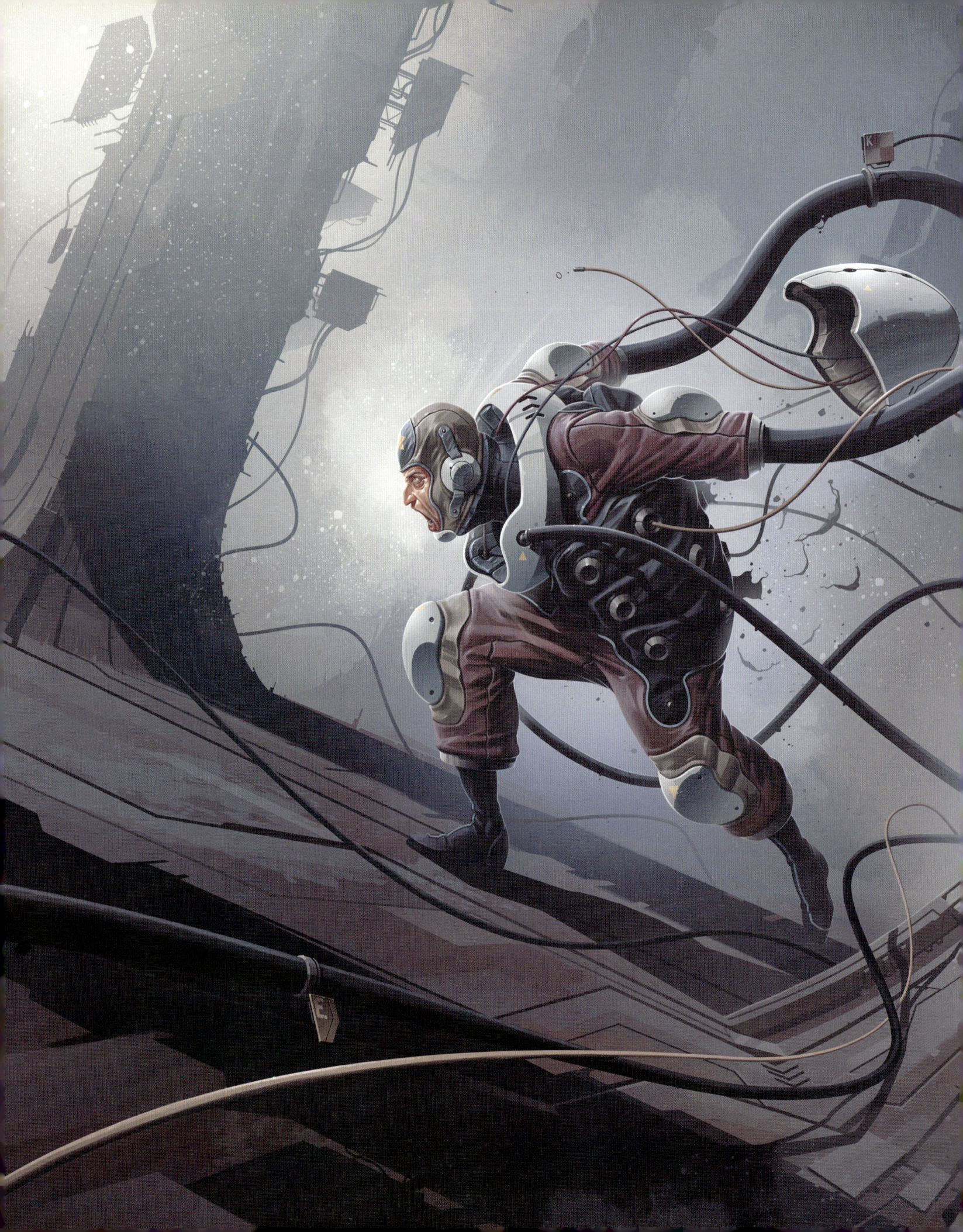

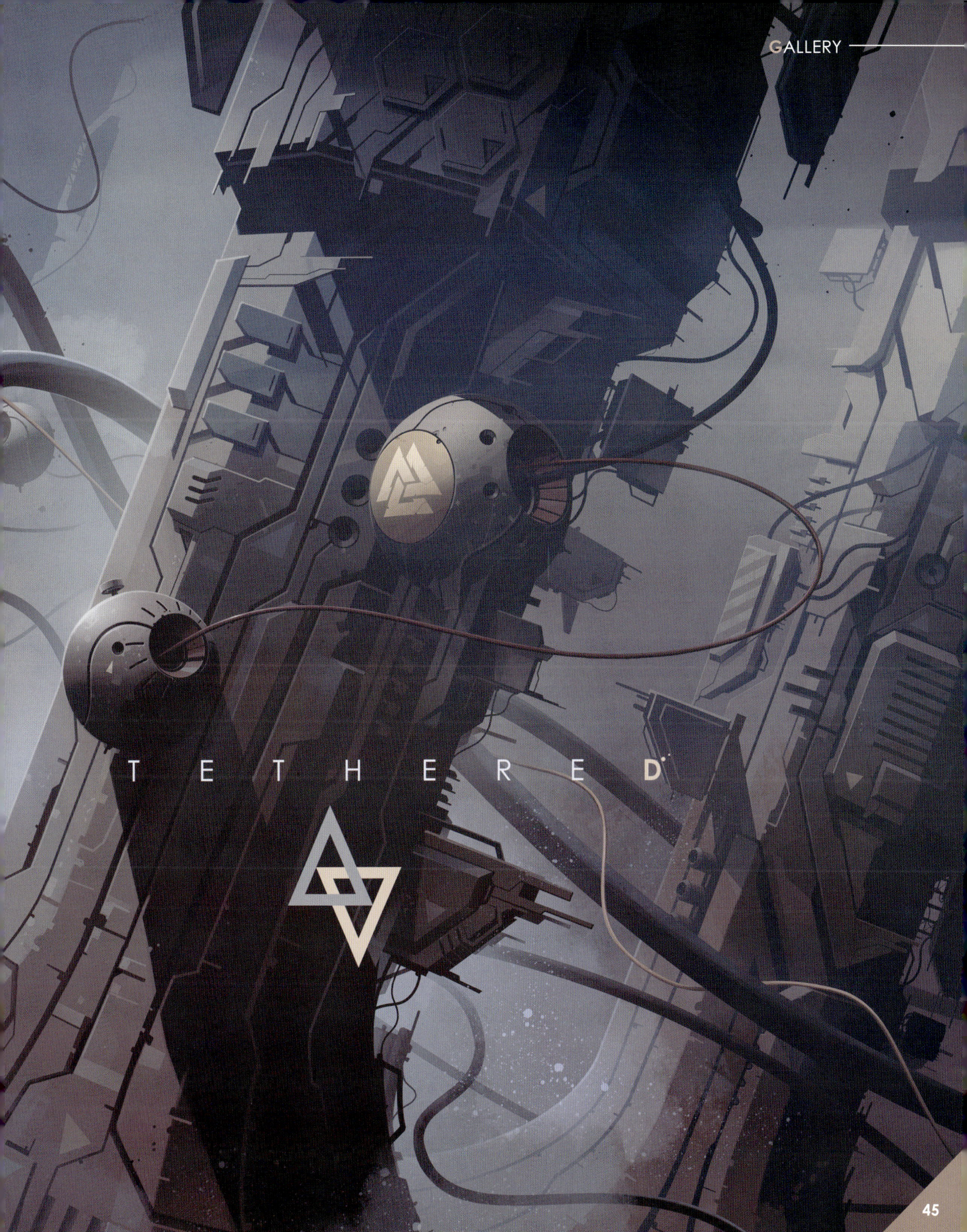

TETHERED

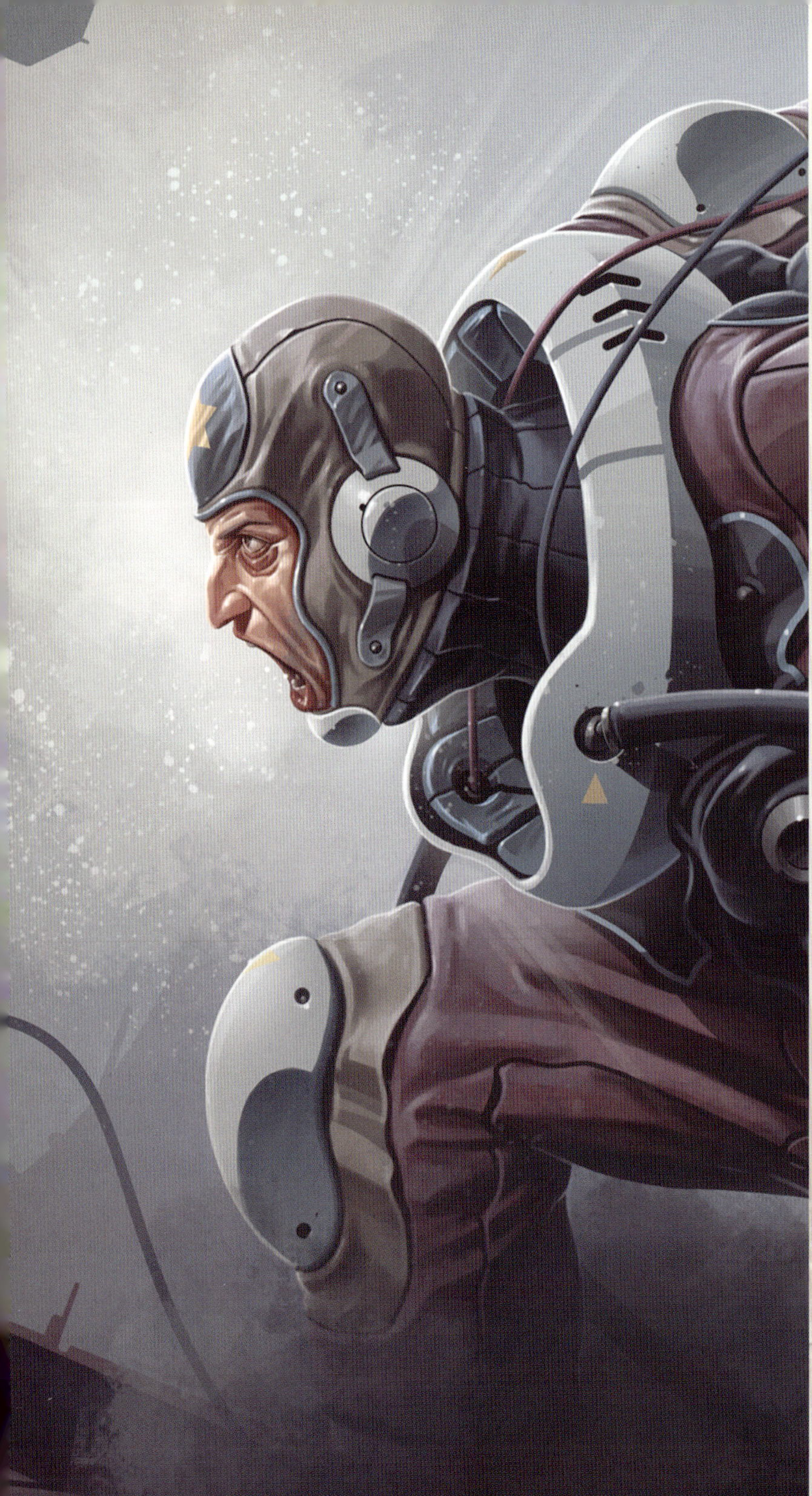

TETHERED ◄◄ p.45/46
2020, 24"x 14"
Graphite, 2D/3D Digital

This one is about being tied or bound, to have your actions or intensions restricted by external forces.

Given everything that was going on in my life at the time... I think this one is pretty self explanatory and sums up my feelings at the time.

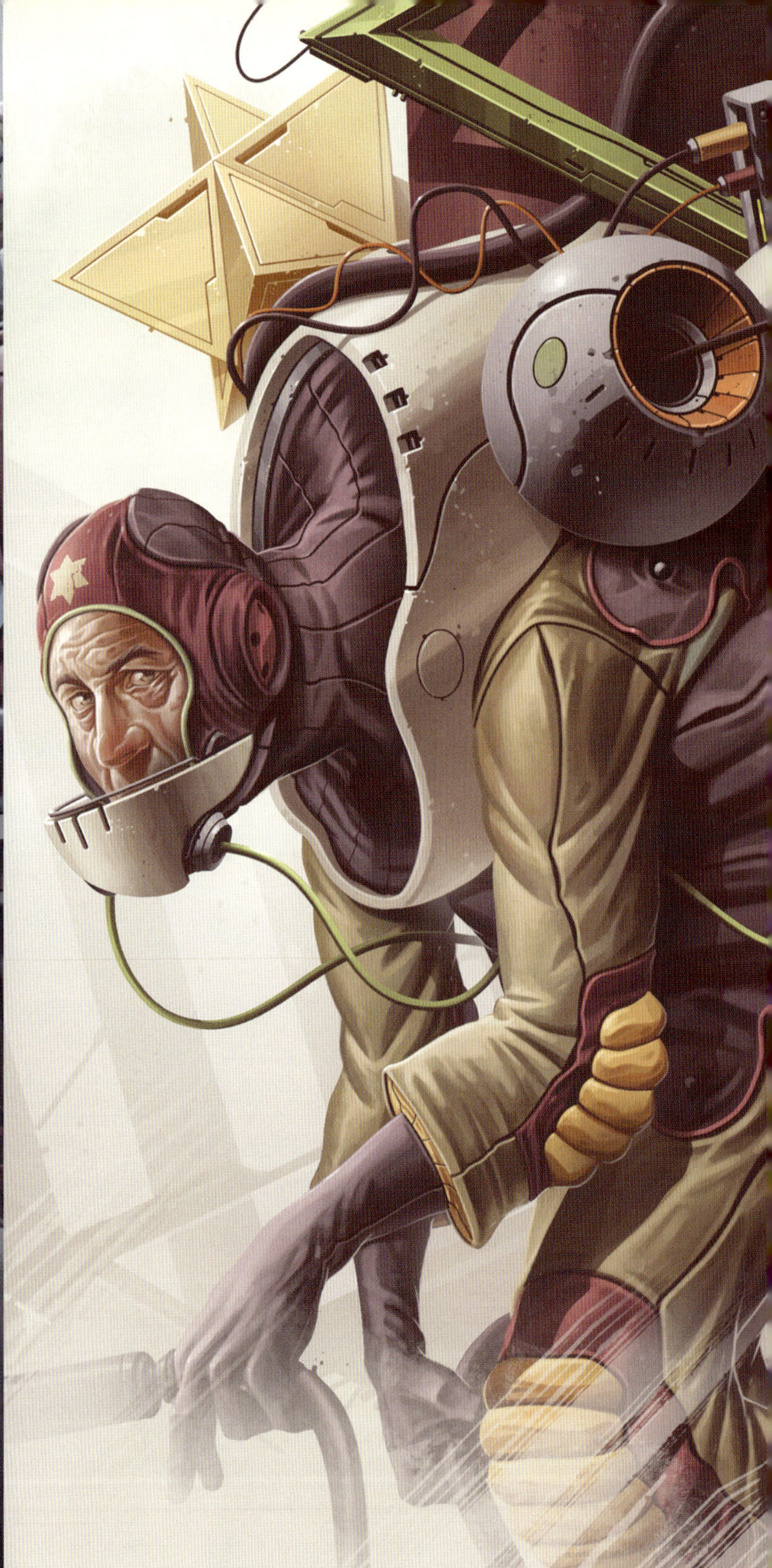

CARRY ►
2020, 16"x 20"
Graphite, 2D/3D Digital

Another piece speaking to the idea of being overloaded and carrying too much weight. All the elements on this old guy's back reference aspects of my life at the time I created the original sketch. I won't go into all that here . . .

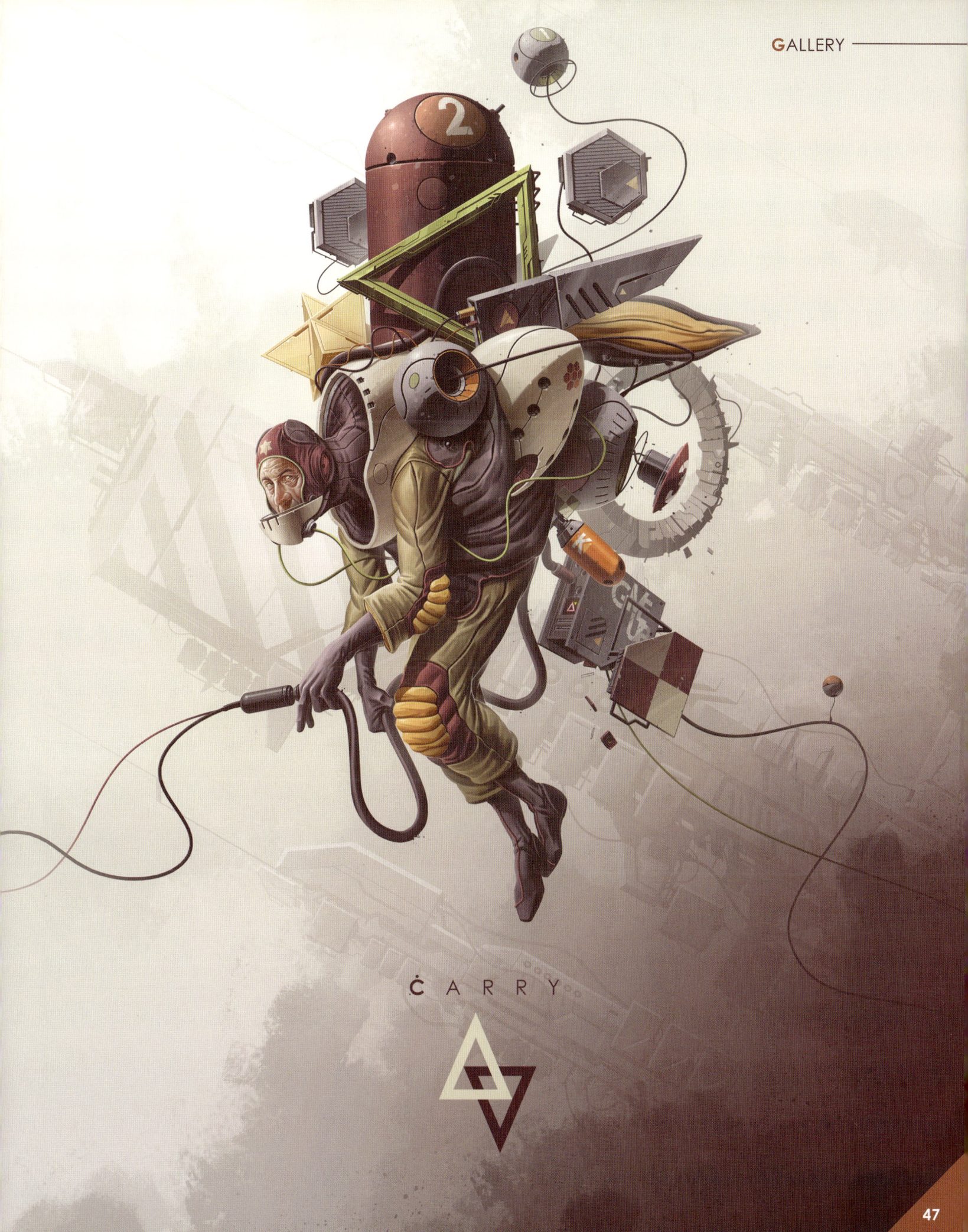

CARRY

MY BODY IS A DYING MACHINE *(memory)*
2020, 24"x 15"
2D/3D Digital

Vascular dementia is a terrible disease. It is a physical process where blood vessels in the brain collapse or become blocked to restrict the delivery of oxygen. Those affected areas of the brain die off and the individual is chipped away until nothing is left.

While my father was now in professional care, he continued his terminal decline . . .

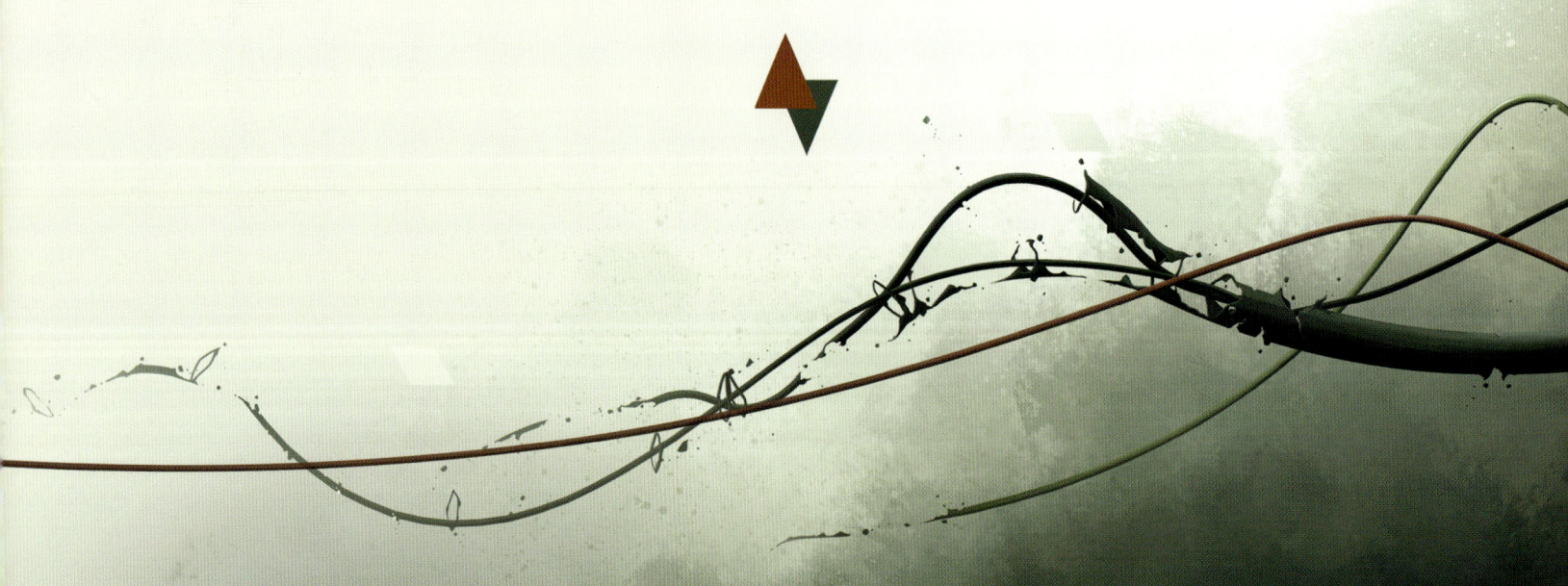

MY BODY IS A DYING MACHINE

erinnerungene

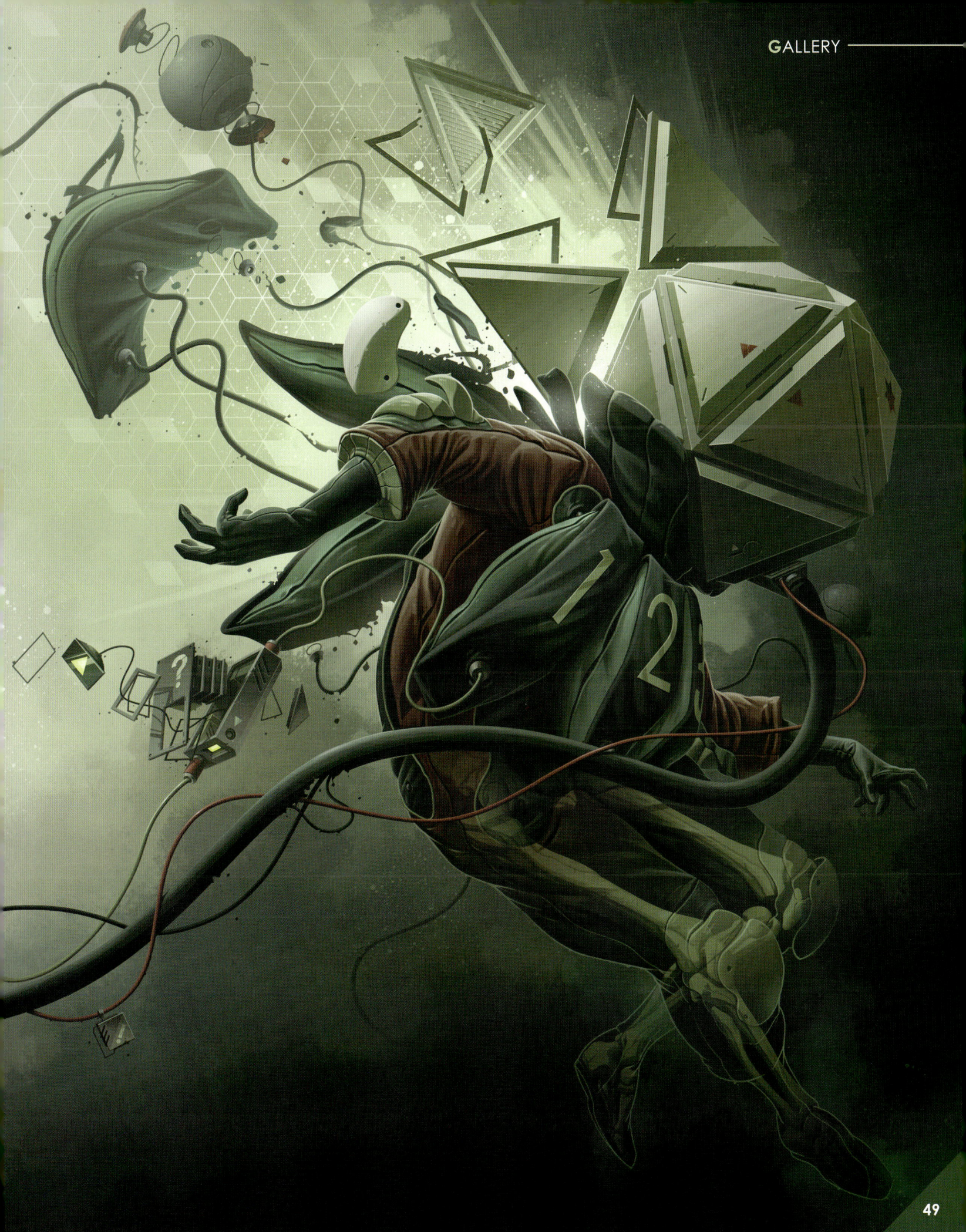

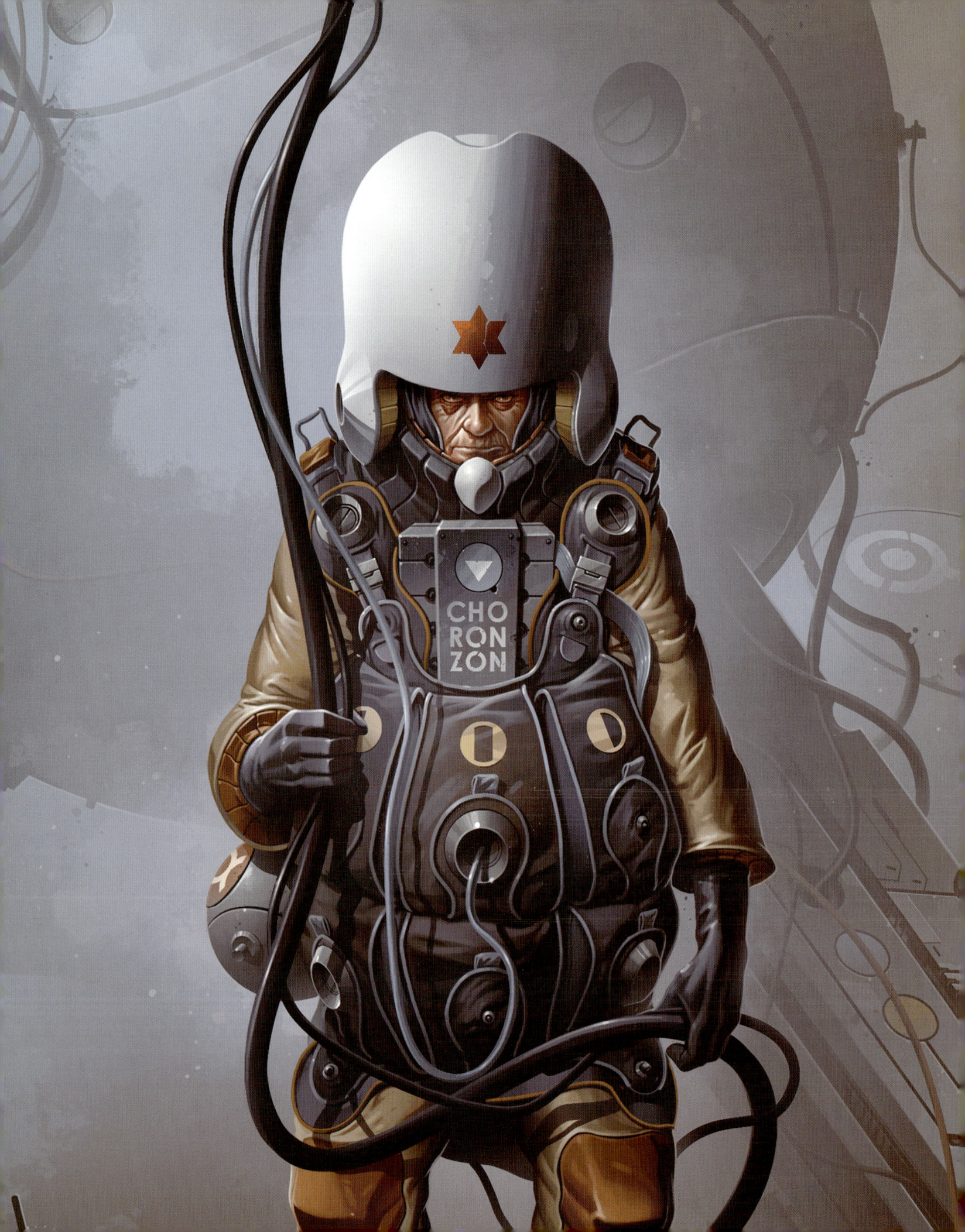

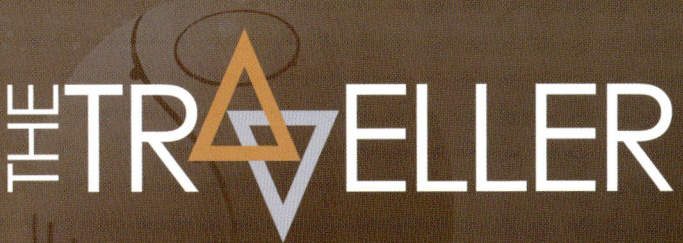

THE TRAVELLER

THE SWORD, THE SERPENT, THE SPEAR

In 2017 I started to talk about creating a fully painted EK sculpture with Ax2 Limited, a small boutique toy company based in Los Angeles. I love the model kits that I do with Industria Mechanika, but I'm not much of a model builder, so my copies of the kits just sit unbuilt in their boxes. For this reason, I always wanted to have a fully assembled, painted figure right out of the box. So, I jumped at the opportunity to move forward with this collaboration. But as my life was pretty chaotic at this time, things moved very slowly.

The design of the figure is informed by concepts borrowed from qabalah. The idea of pathways on the Tree of Life that pertain to the release and return of divine/creative energies are concepts that I have often seen as representative of artistic inspiration, and the efforts of the artist to harness and use that inspiration. So, the Traveller figure is meant to symbolize the Tree of Life, and the three colour forms of the figure relate to these three pathways: the Sword, the Serpent, and the Spear.

Sculpting of the figure was handled by the talented Leo Haslam. I had seen Leo's work on ArtStation, and I was immediately impressed. I love his attention to detail, and his experience sculpting for 3D printed figures was a bonus. The Ax2 production team then took Leo's sculpt and printed and painted an amazing looking prototype figure.

By the time the design and sculpting were done we had decided to try and run this project as a Kickstarter. This was something none of us had done before, so it took some time to get it all organized. So, after a protracted development period, The Traveller resin statue project finally launched on Kickstarter in the fall of 2021. The project was fully funded and deliveries of the statues and other related reward items commenced in 2022.

The following pages feature the production paintings for the three forms of the Traveller, as well as images of Leo's awesome sculpt and Ax2's amazing prototype figure.

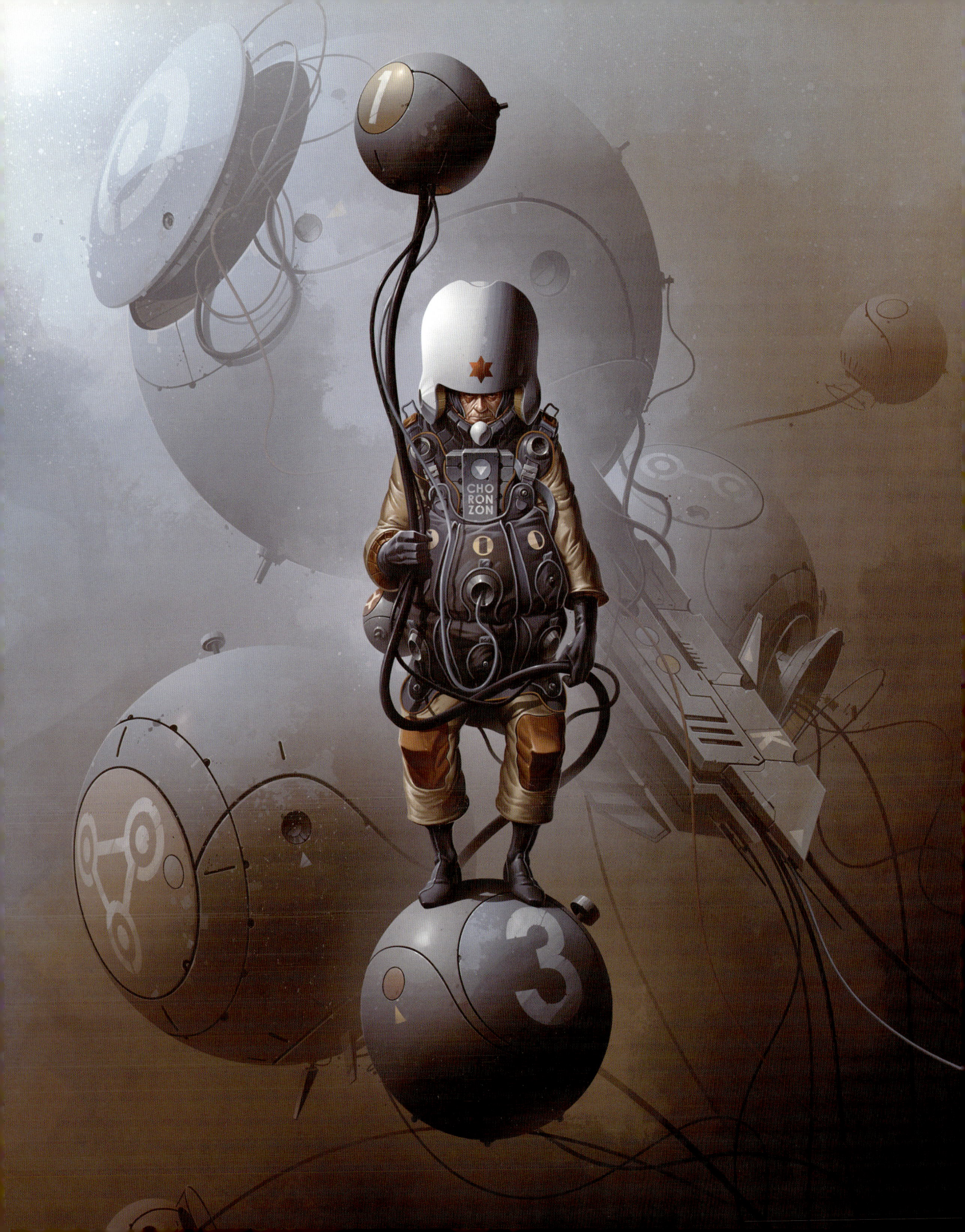

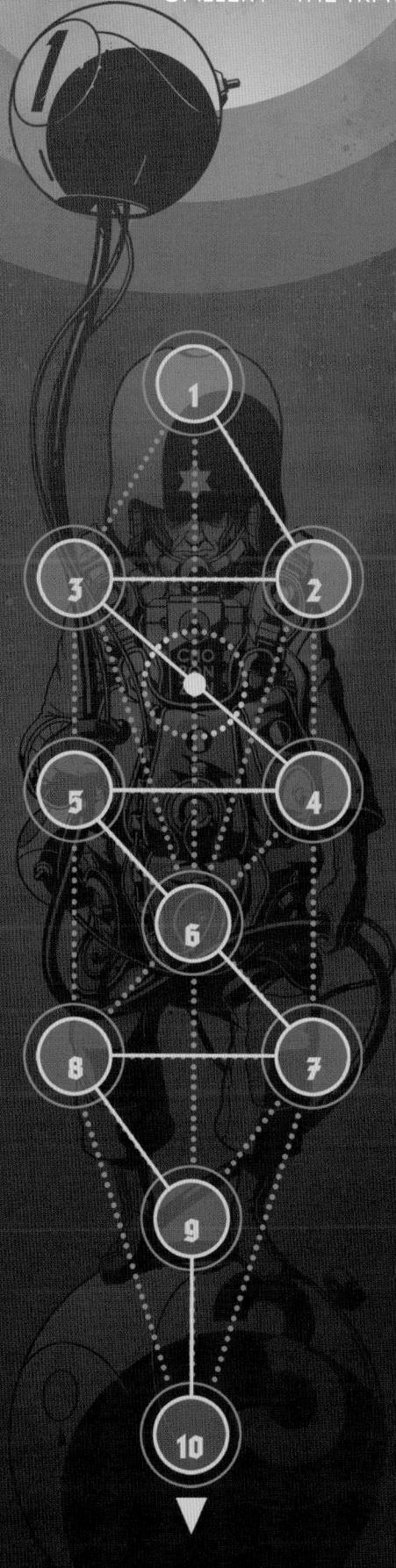

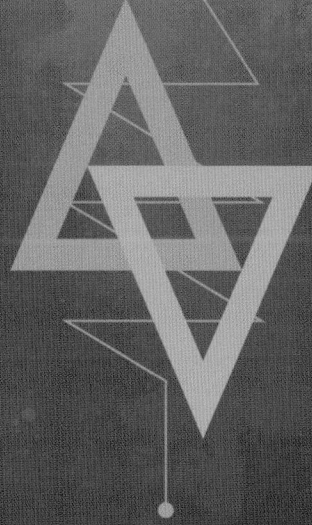

THE SWORD

This colour variation of the Traveller represents the flash of creative inspiration, the downward flow of creative energy, the Path of the Sword. While the source of this inspiration, or sudden "flash" can be from a mix of external stimuli, an emotional outpouring, or something bubbling up from the subconscious, I'm willing to accept "creative energy" as a metaphor for these different origins. The blue downward triangle points in the direction of the energy transfer, and it also represents the chalice, the receptive vessel for this inspiration, the artist.

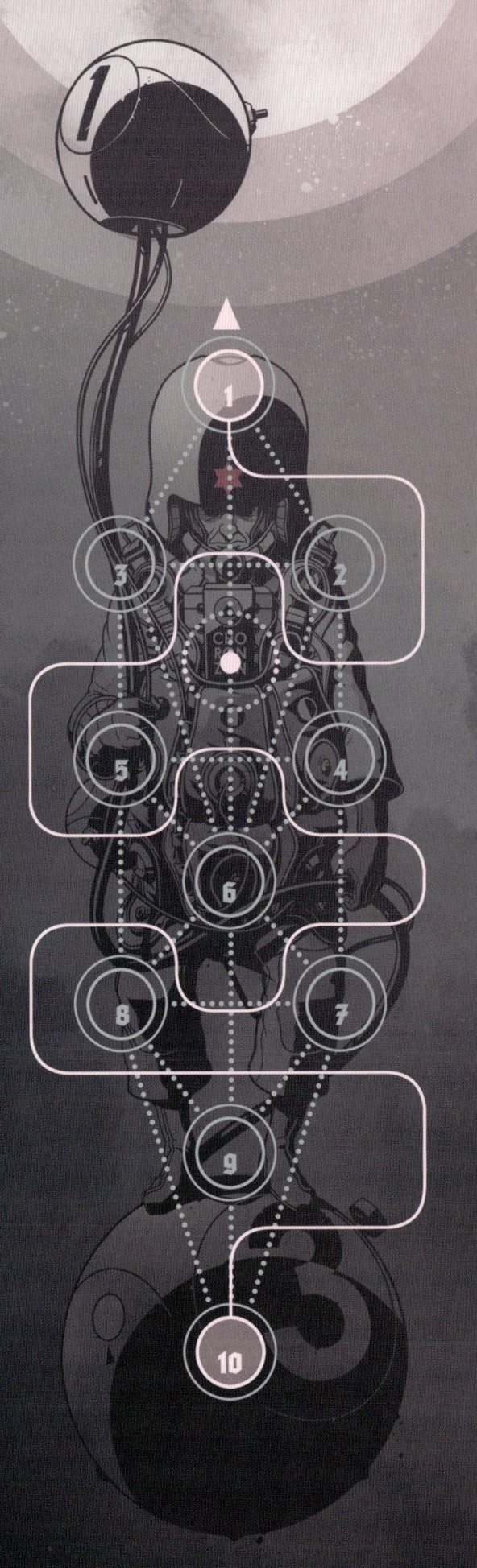

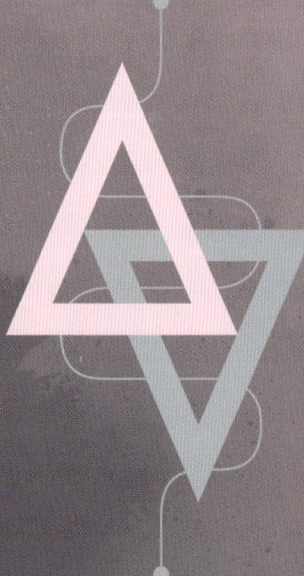

THE SERPENT

This form of the Traveller is the first of the two possible paths of return - the effort of the artist to use this inspiration to create something in the material world. The Path of the Serpent is an upward winding path, representing a long and potentially arduous journey to the final outcome. For me, this is an art piece that requires a lot of reworking and struggle to complete (as this one was). The pink upward pointing triangle (the blade) is meant to represent the aspiration of the artist reaching back to the source of inspiration.

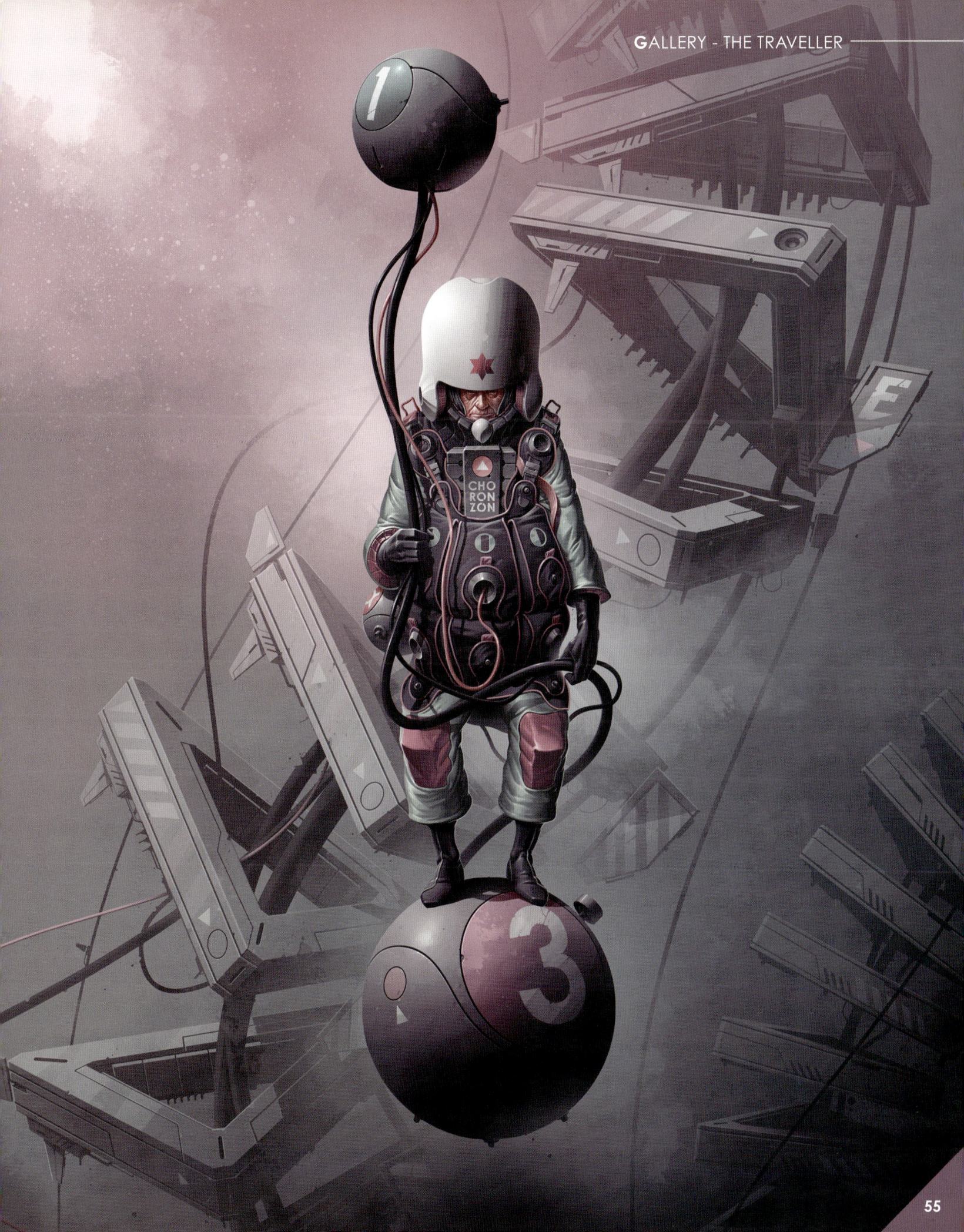

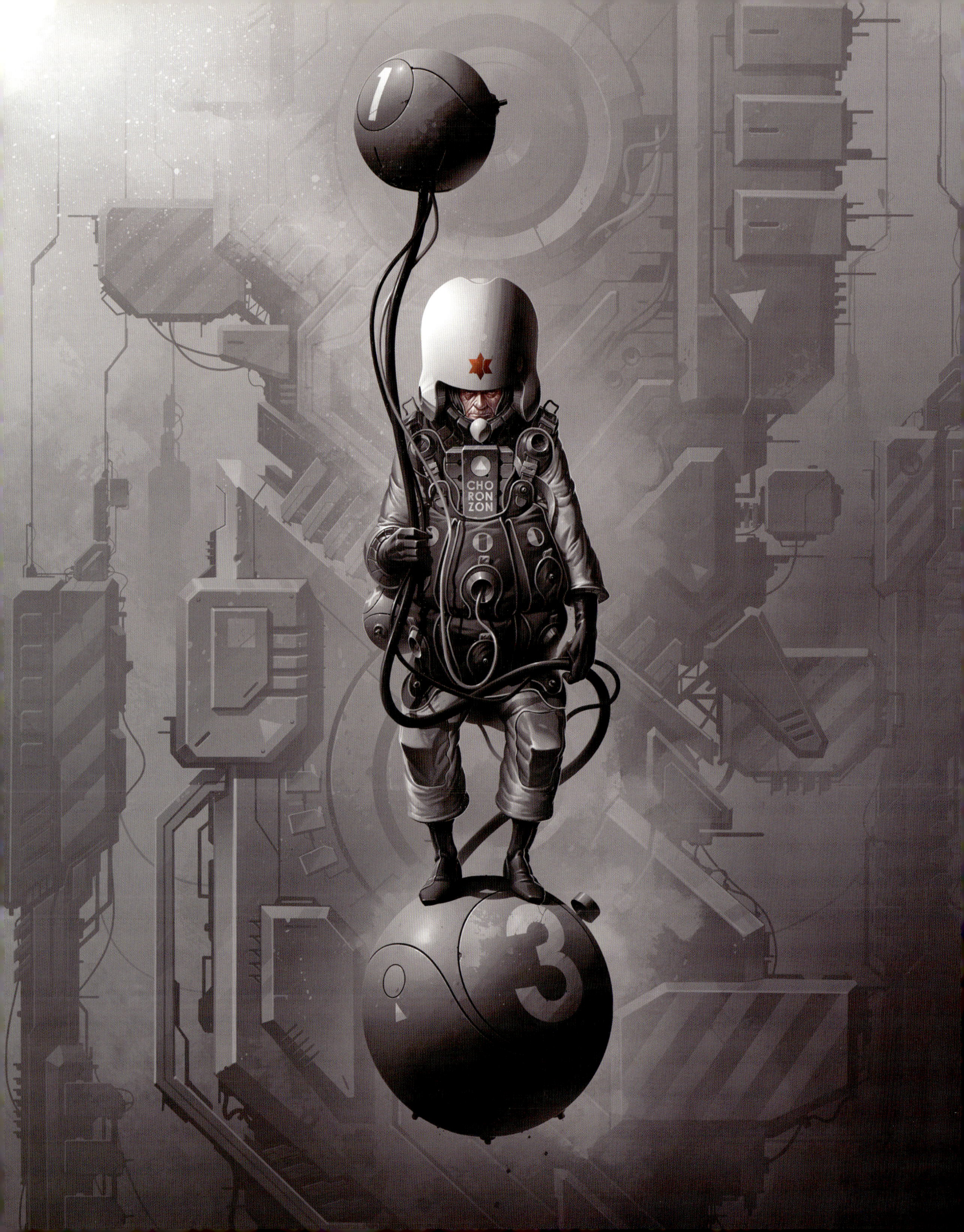

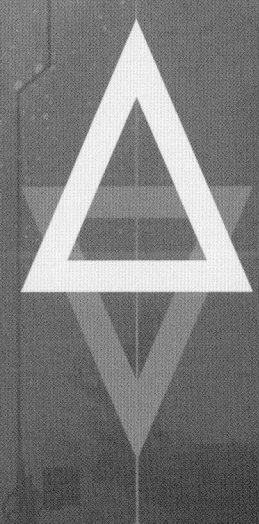

THE SPEAR

The final version of the Traveller, and the second possible path of return, the Path of the Spear. In qabalah this path (called the Path of the Arrow) shoots straight up the middle of the Tree, the Path of Illumination, a kind of shortcut for those who have attained cosmic consciousness. For me, this symbolizes the creation of a piece where everything seems to just flow and come together with little effort—a straight shot to a final piece that I'm happy with.

Leo Haslam, a sculptor from the UK, was brought in to do the modelling on the master sculpt. It was interesting to see his interpretation of the "EK Style," as it was different from Gene's work. I think he really did a really good job of capturing the feeling/attitude of the original artwork.

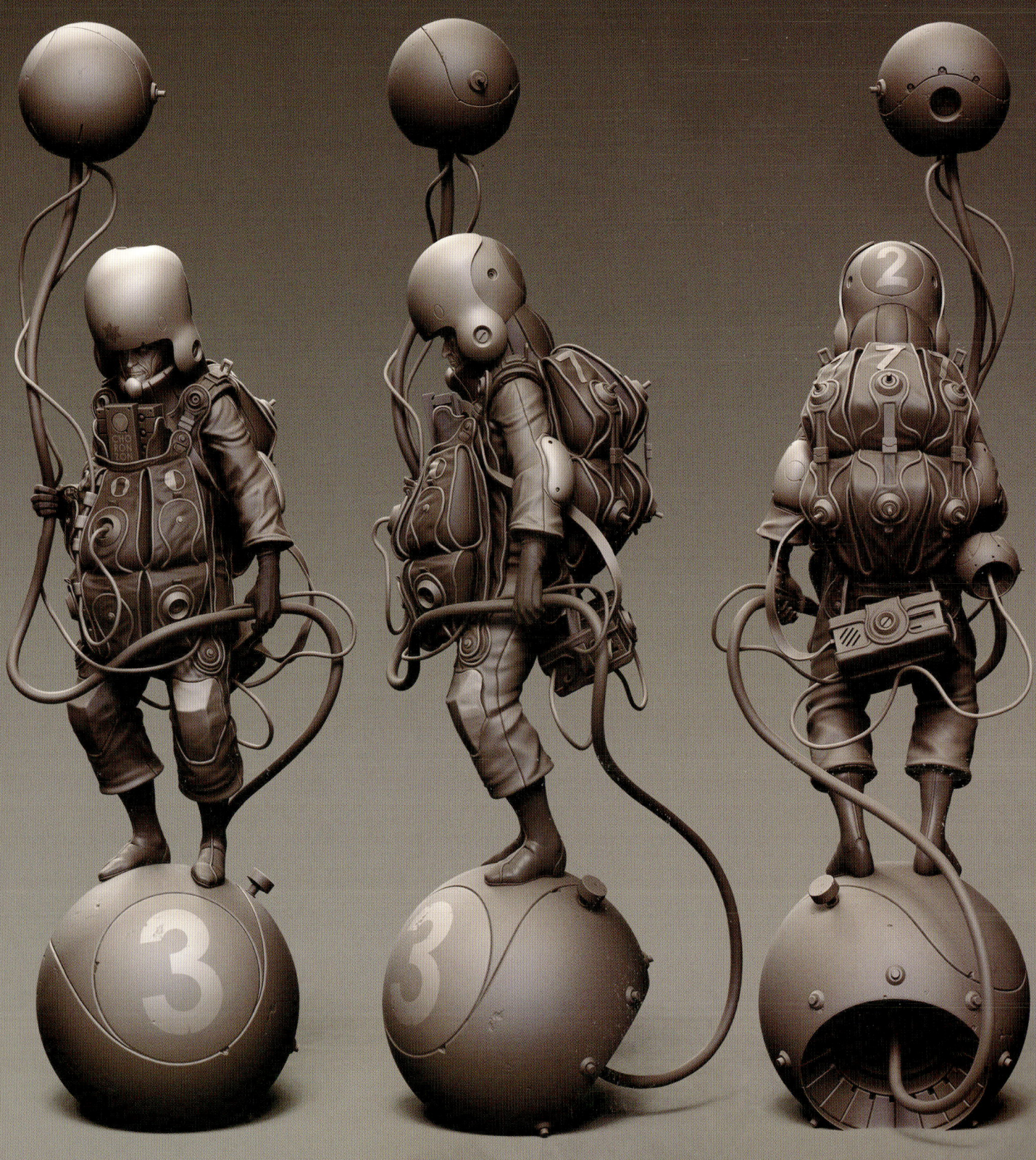

Traveller Sculpt Render - Final | Leo Haslam | Jun. 06, 2020

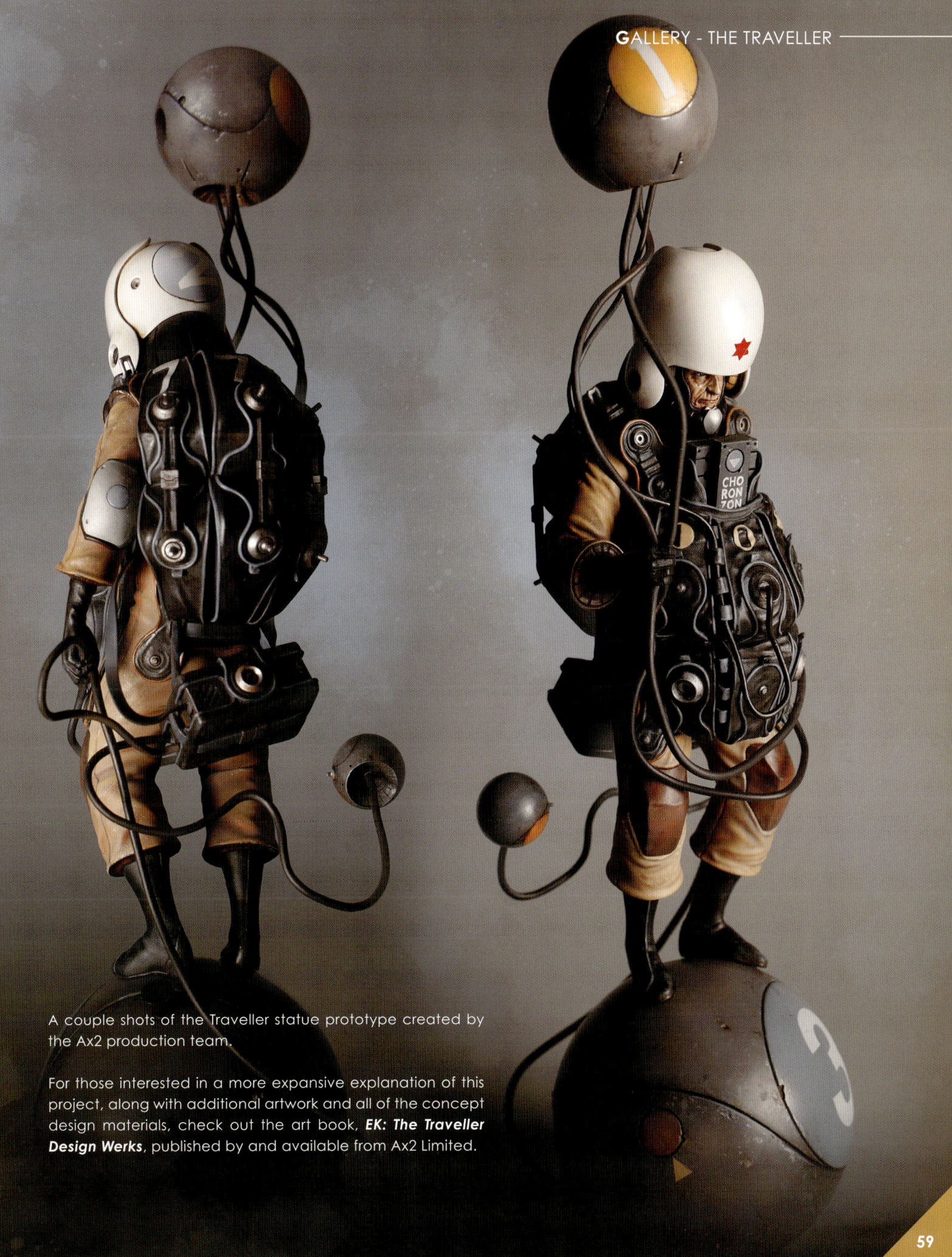

A couple shots of the Traveller statue prototype created by the Ax2 production team.

For those interested in a more expansive explanation of this project, along with additional artwork and all of the concept design materials, check out the art book, *EK: The Traveller Design Werks*, published by and available from Ax2 Limited.

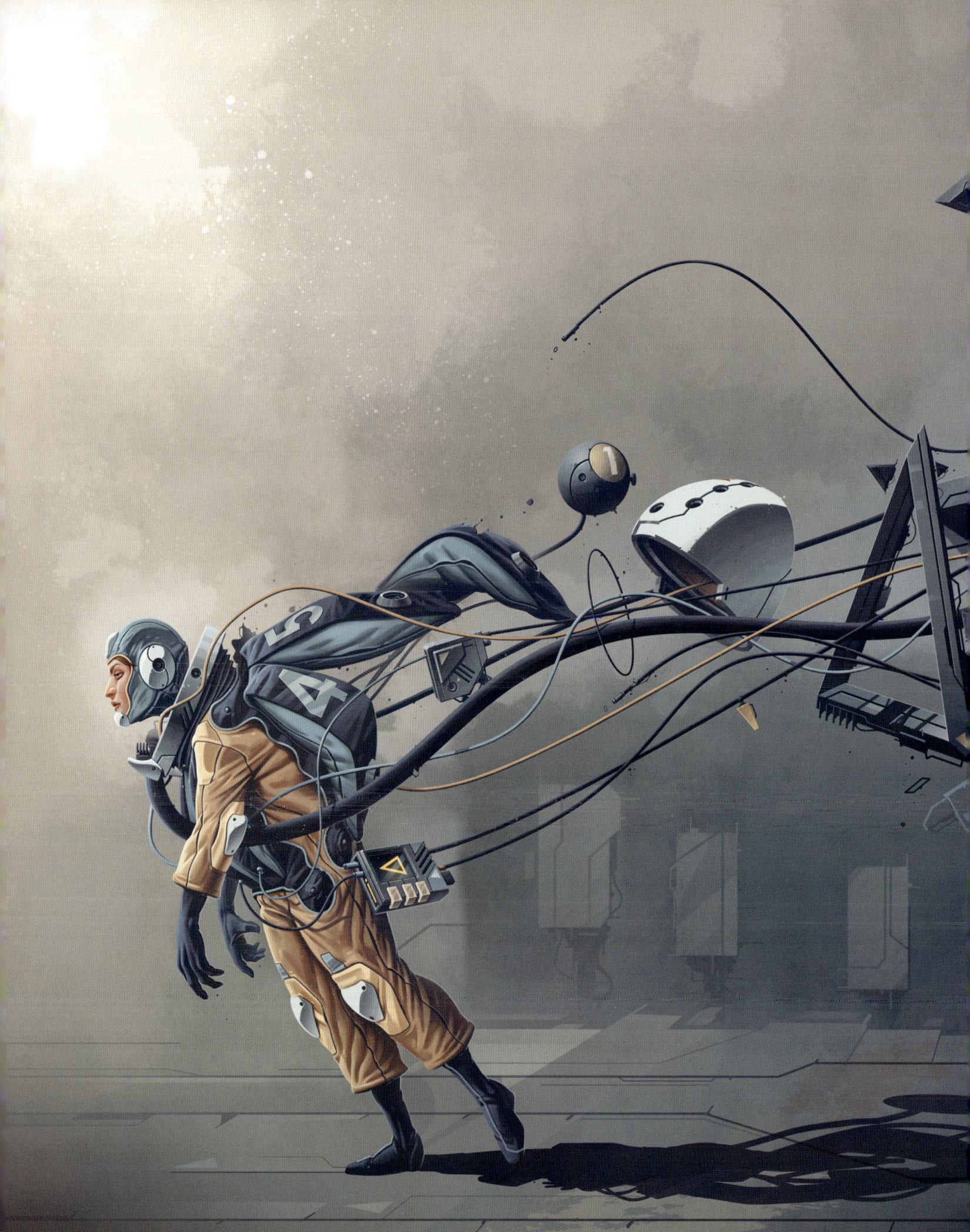

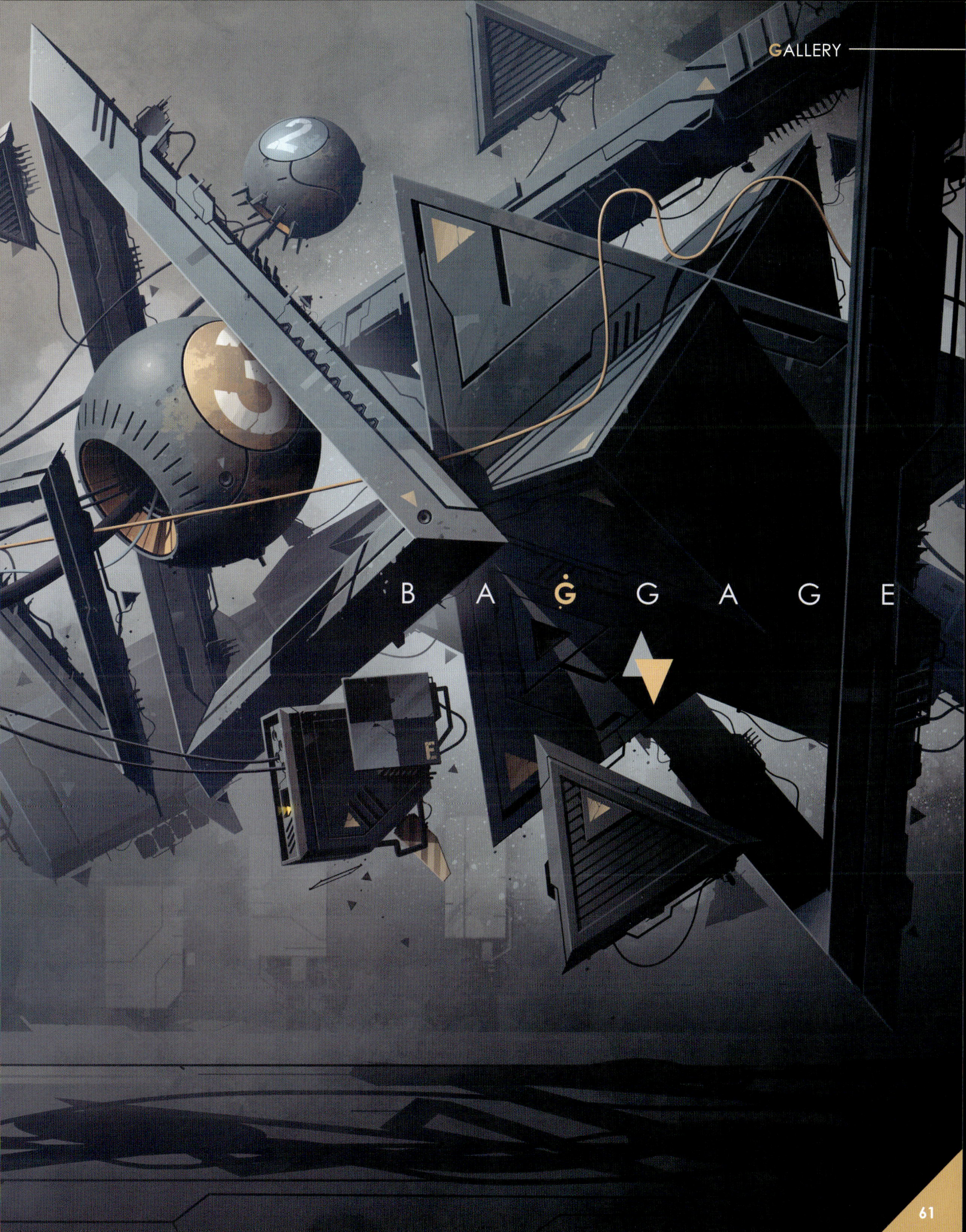

BAGGAGE

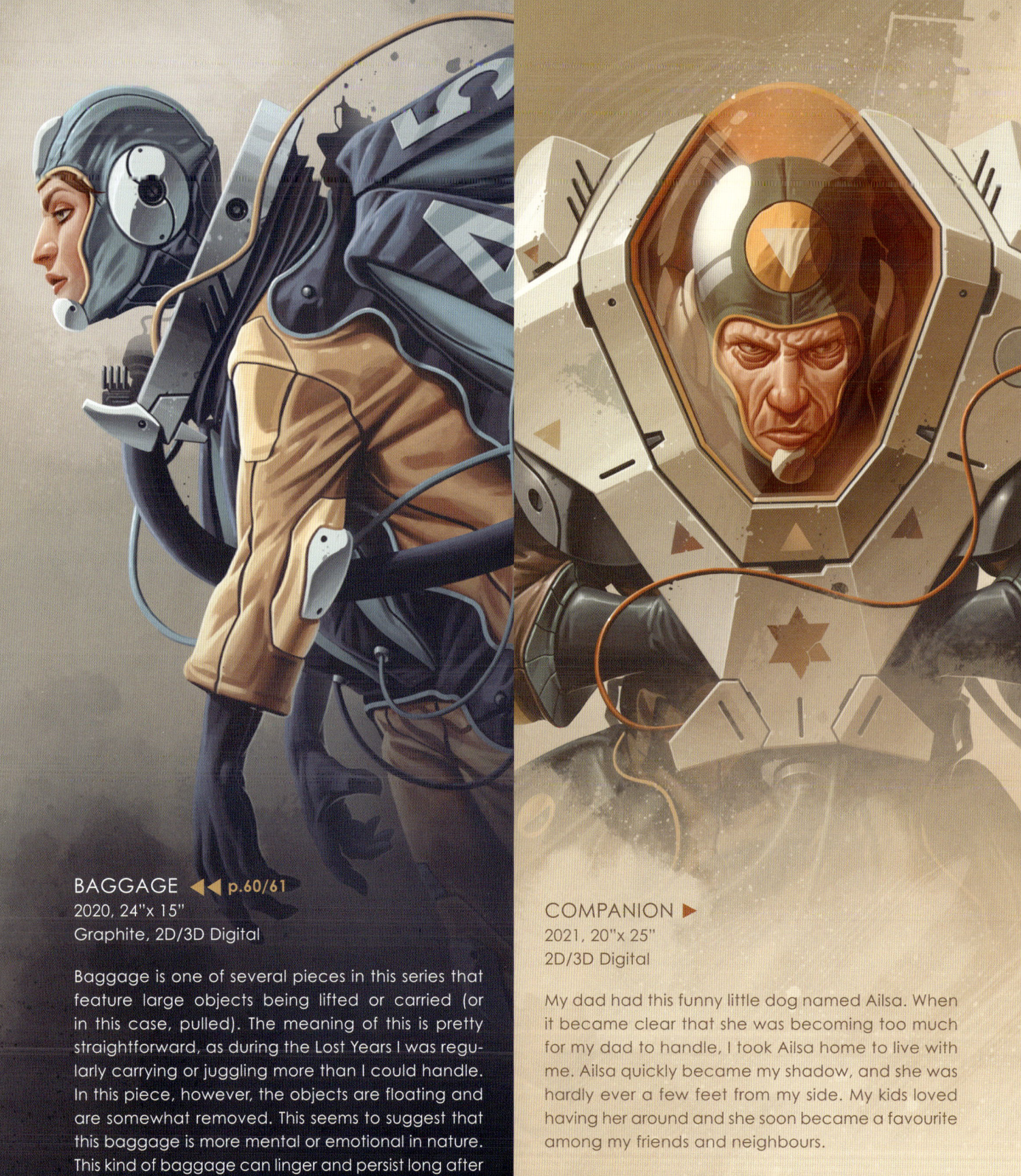

BAGGAGE ◀◀ p.60/61
2020, 24"x 15"
Graphite, 2D/3D Digital

Baggage is one of several pieces in this series that feature large objects being lifted or carried (or in this case, pulled). The meaning of this is pretty straightforward, as during the Lost Years I was regularly carrying or juggling more than I could handle. In this piece, however, the objects are floating and are somewhat removed. This seems to suggest that this baggage is more mental or emotional in nature. This kind of baggage can linger and persist long after physical hardships have passed. Some people say that everything heals with time. Given that a couple of those connecting wires have already snapped, it should only be a matter of time until all of this baggage is released.

COMPANION ▶
2021, 20"x 25"
2D/3D Digital

My dad had this funny little dog named Ailsa. When it became clear that she was becoming too much for my dad to handle, I took Ailsa home to live with me. Ailsa quickly became my shadow, and she was hardly ever a few feet from my side. My kids loved having her around and she soon became a favourite among my friends and neighbours.

Unfortunately, she developed cancer, and when her bad days started to outweigh the good days, we made the decision to put her down. We were lucky to have two and a half great years with Ailsa. She will be missed.

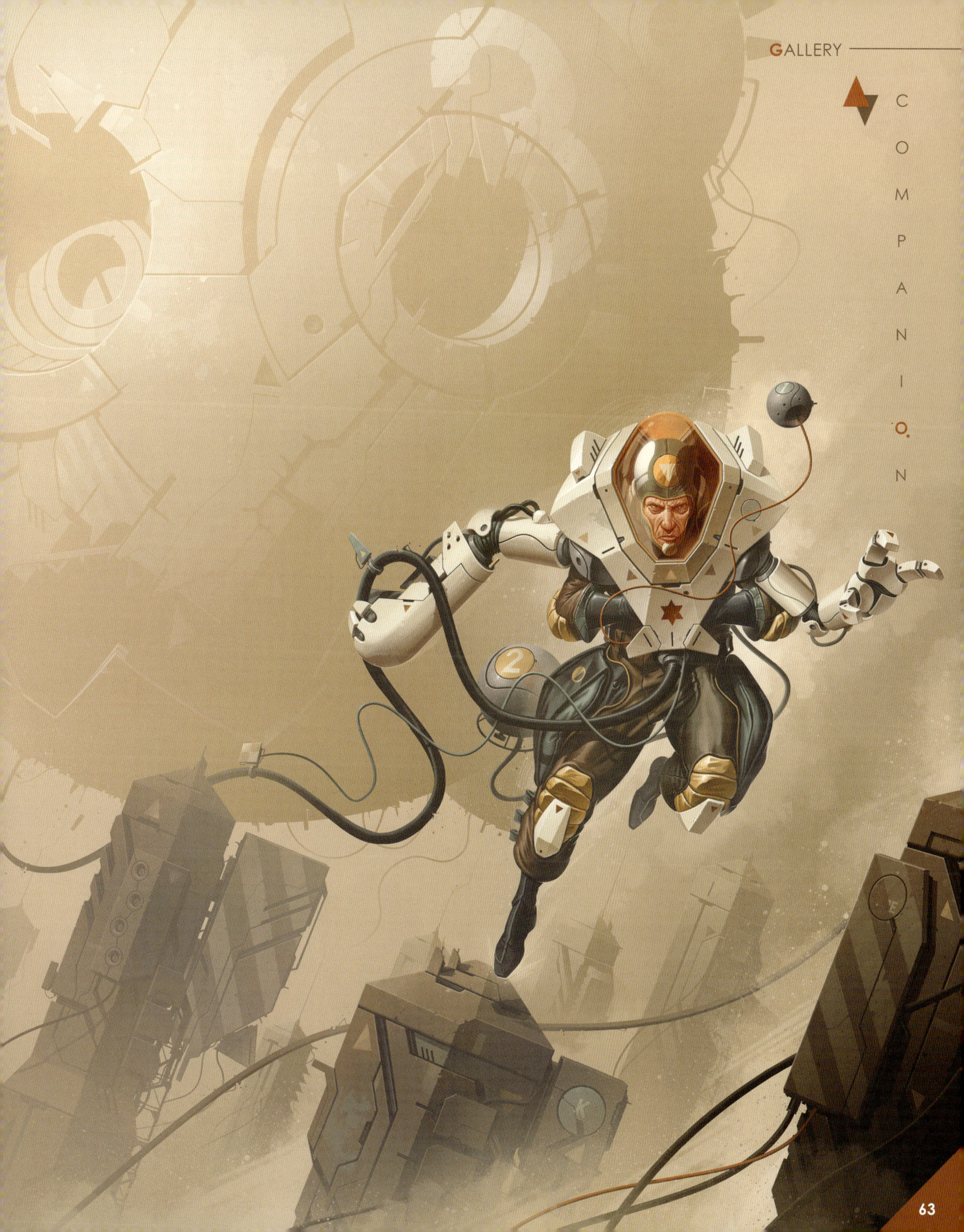

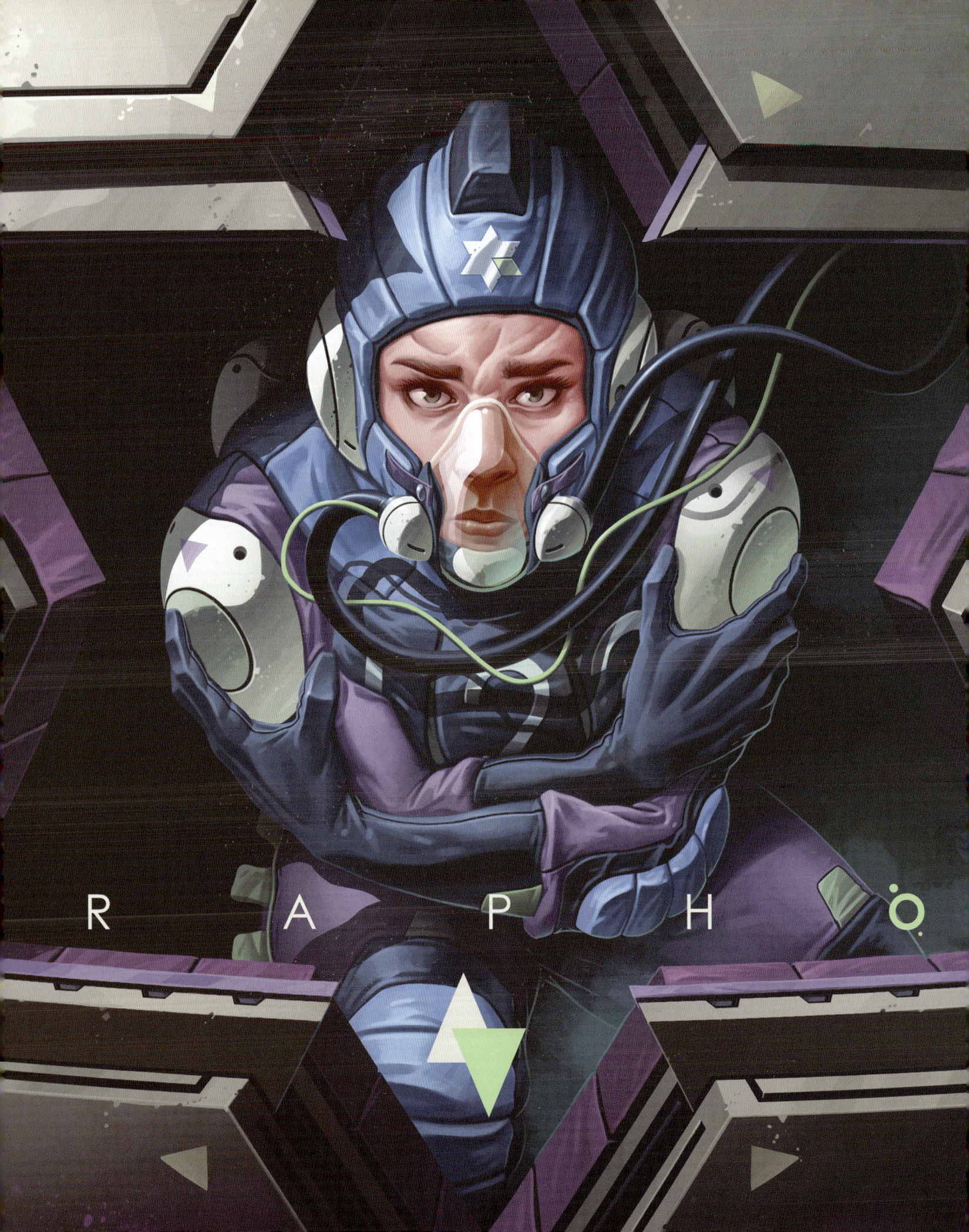

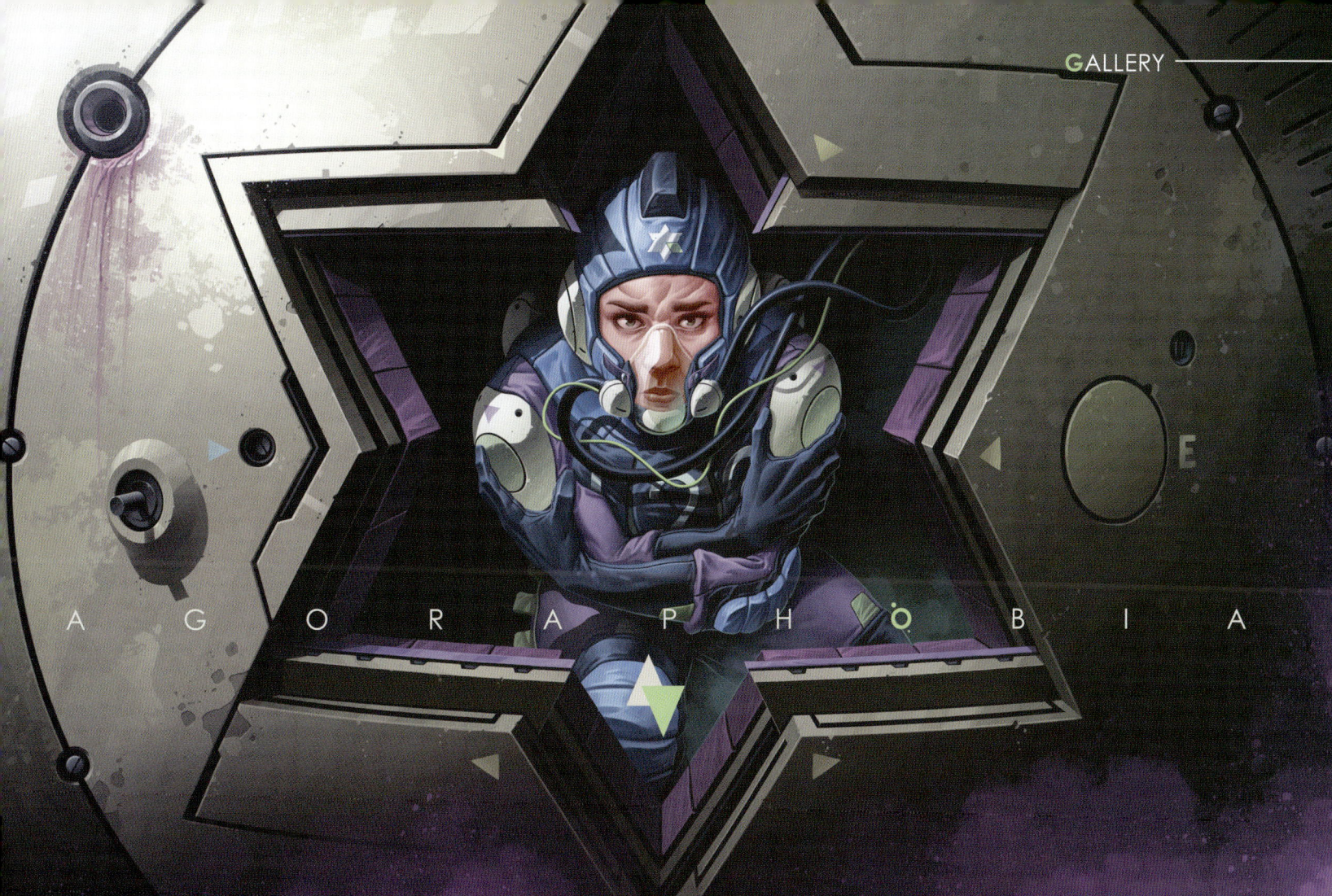

AGORAPHOBIA

I'm no spring chicken, so in my life I can remember big events like the fall of the Berlin Wall and the collapse of the Soviet system; 9/11 and US/Western reactions to it; the rise of the Internet and digital culture, etc. But this Covid-19 pandemic felt a little different. Maybe because it was truly global, or maybe it could be that I'm just older now and have a different perspective on things - or it could be that it affected my children's lives, and this heightened the perceived threat of it all. Anyway, I usually don't create EK pieces that reflect current events, but I ended up creating a couple pieces that, in retrospect, can only be seen as reactions to the pandemic.

Let's hope it is another 100 years before the next big one!

◀ **AGORAPHOBIA**
2020, 13"x 11"
2D/3D Digital

This one speaks to early times in the pandemic, when we didn't know how serious or infectious the virus/disease was, and even leaving the house was accompanied with a feeling of uncertainty.

▶▶ **p.66** COMFORT ZONE
(shelter in place)
2020, 16"x 20"
2D/3D Digital

I'm a bit of a hermit by nature, so when quarantine hit it didn't seem to bother me too much. We also got off pretty easy, as the pandemic didn't affect my job, and our schools, restaurants, and businesses largely remained open. That being said, I'm in no hurry to go back into lockdown - even if there is another pandemic.

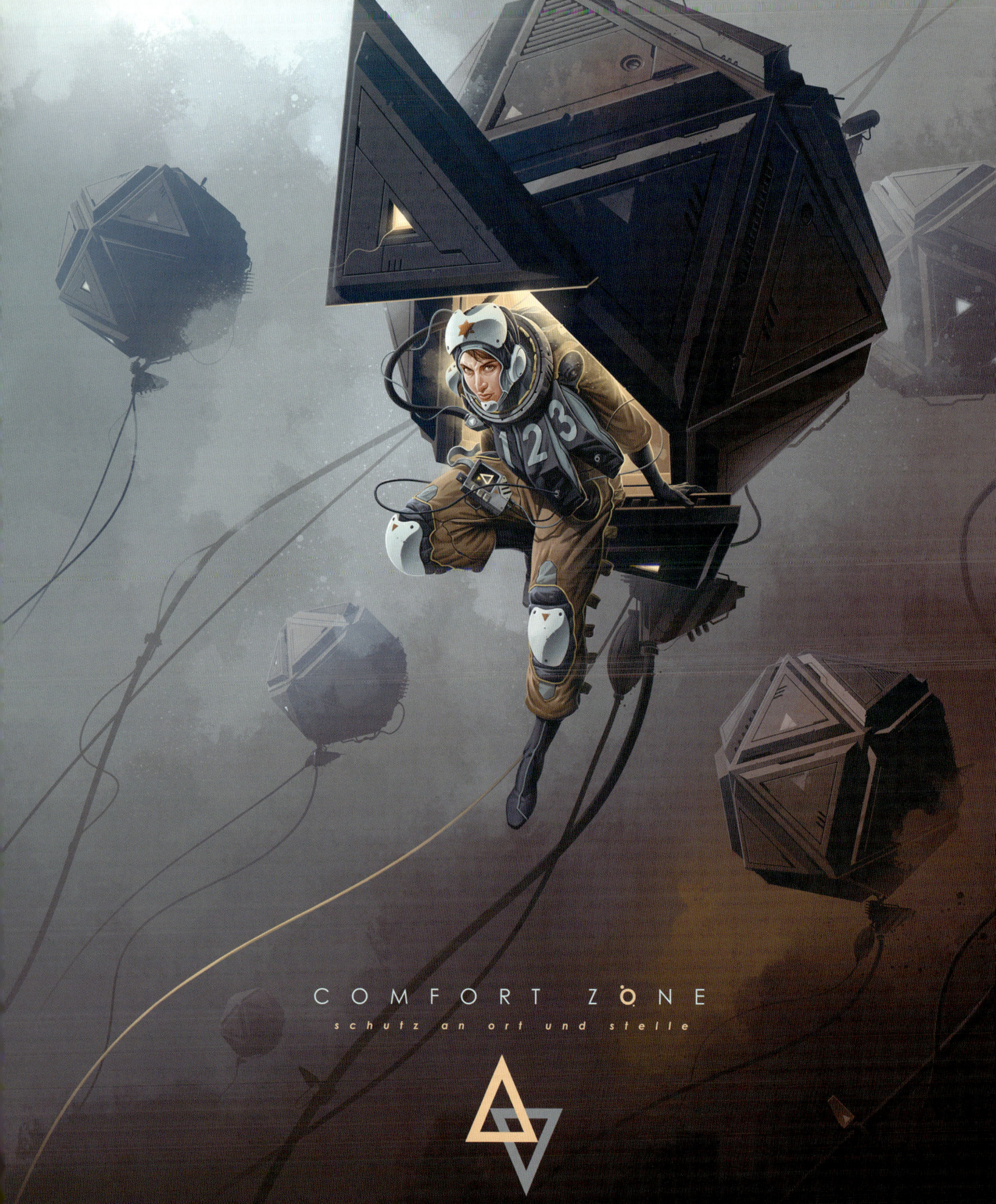

COMFORT ZONE

schutz an ort und stelle

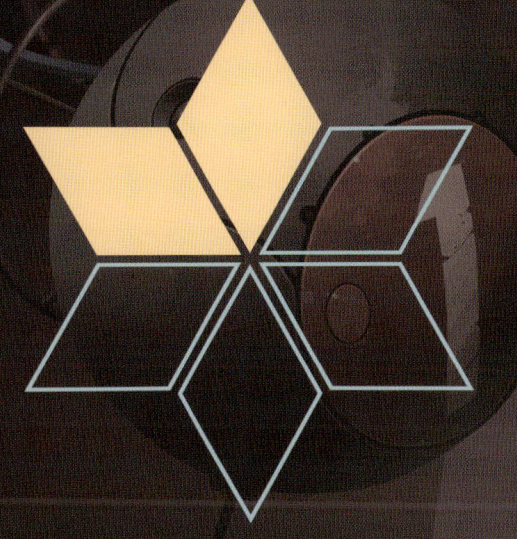

TWO FOUR SERIES

In 2019, after the launch of the Duchess kit, Michael at Industria Mechanika asked me if I would be interested in producing a line of smaller EK model kits. Since things were calming down for me in both my personal life and on the work front, I thought that this would be a great project to get me back to working on some of my own artwork. I reworked a few of the sketches that I had done in the preceding years into several design options that I presented to Industria Mechanika. In typical fashion, Michael wanted to do them all, and we decided that we would do them in 1/24 scale. So, I began to expand these designs into larger, more detailed paintings and to create more detailed design materials to aid in the sculpting of the kits.

With Gene out of the picture, we had to find a new modeller. Michael and I both had contacts that we thought would be good for this project, and after discussing it, we settled on a modeller that we both really liked, and this person agreed to take on the project. Unfortunately, that is when things started to go sideways. Progress on the sculpt was slow, really slow. I realize that this was a side project, and people have more important things to focus on, like their personal lives and work (I treat this EK stuff in the same way). But we would go months without any updates, and I found myself having to create more design materials than usual to communicate the vision of the pieces. After about a year, the first sculpt was still incomplete, and then things just trailed off, with emails left unanswered and no more updates at all.

cont. p.68

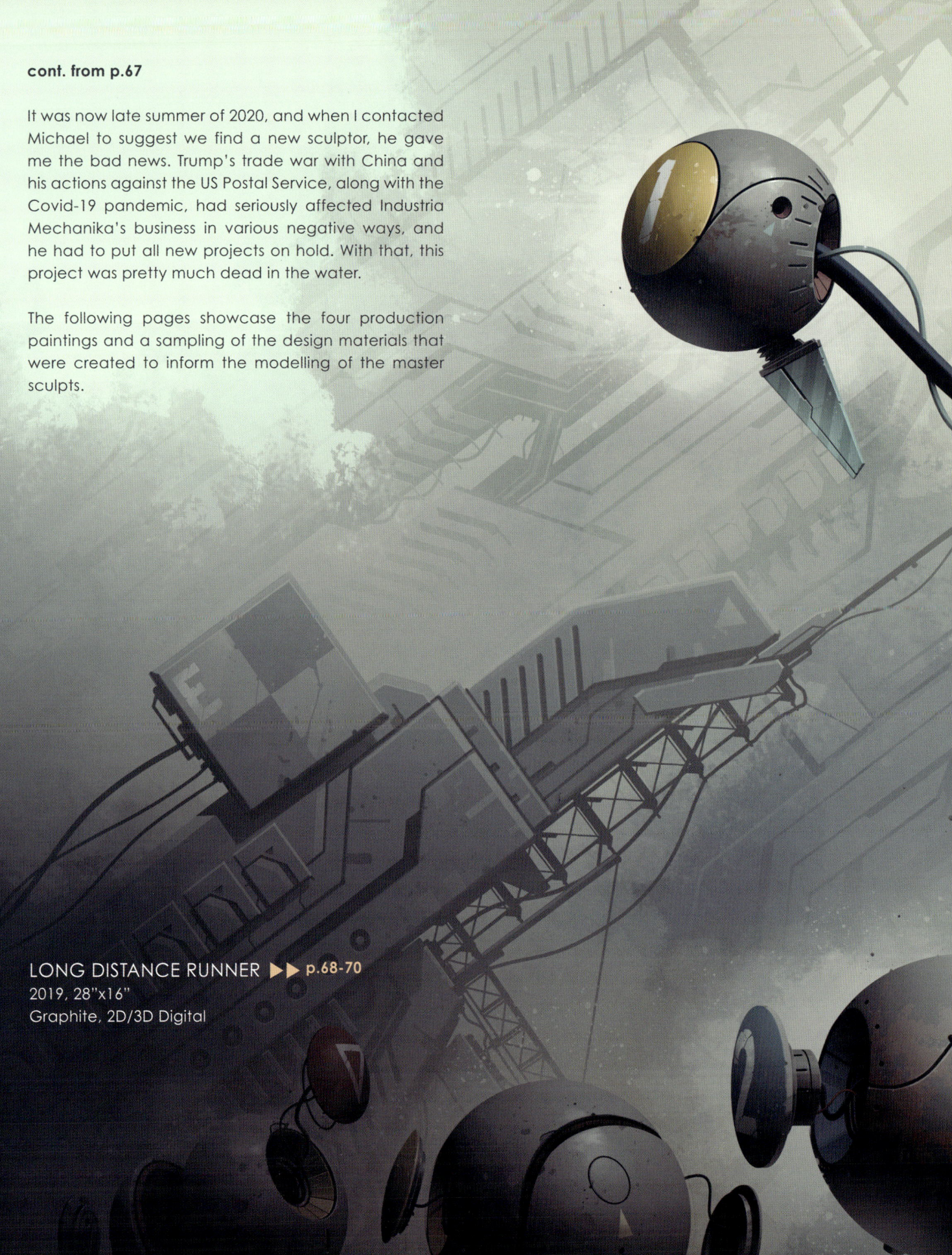

cont. from p.67

It was now late summer of 2020, and when I contacted Michael to suggest we find a new sculptor, he gave me the bad news. Trump's trade war with China and his actions against the US Postal Service, along with the Covid-19 pandemic, had seriously affected Industria Mechanika's business in various negative ways, and he had to put all new projects on hold. With that, this project was pretty much dead in the water.

The following pages showcase the four production paintings and a sampling of the design materials that were created to inform the modelling of the master sculpts.

LONG DISTANCE RUNNER ▶▶ p.68-70
2019, 28"x16"
Graphite, 2D/3D Digital

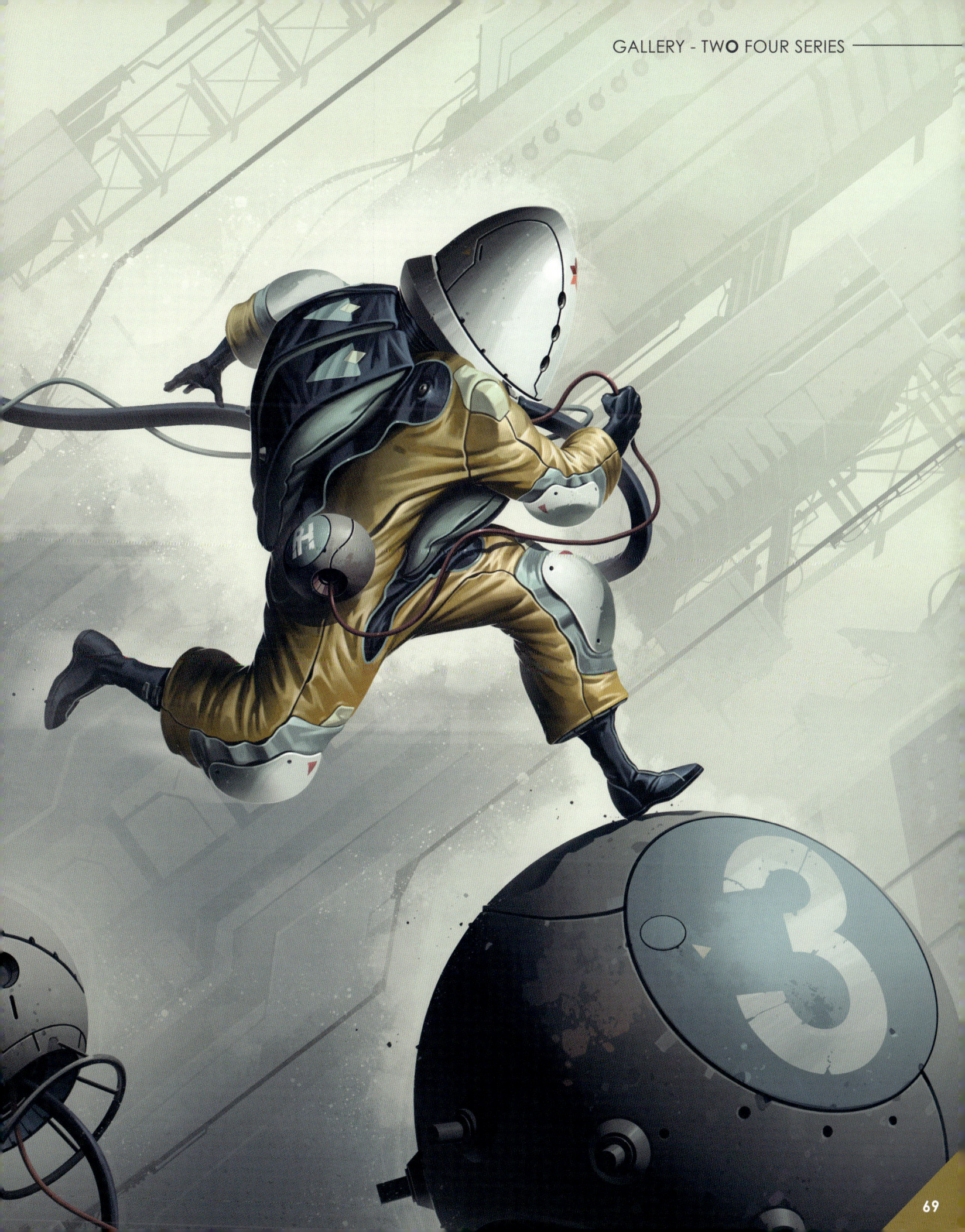

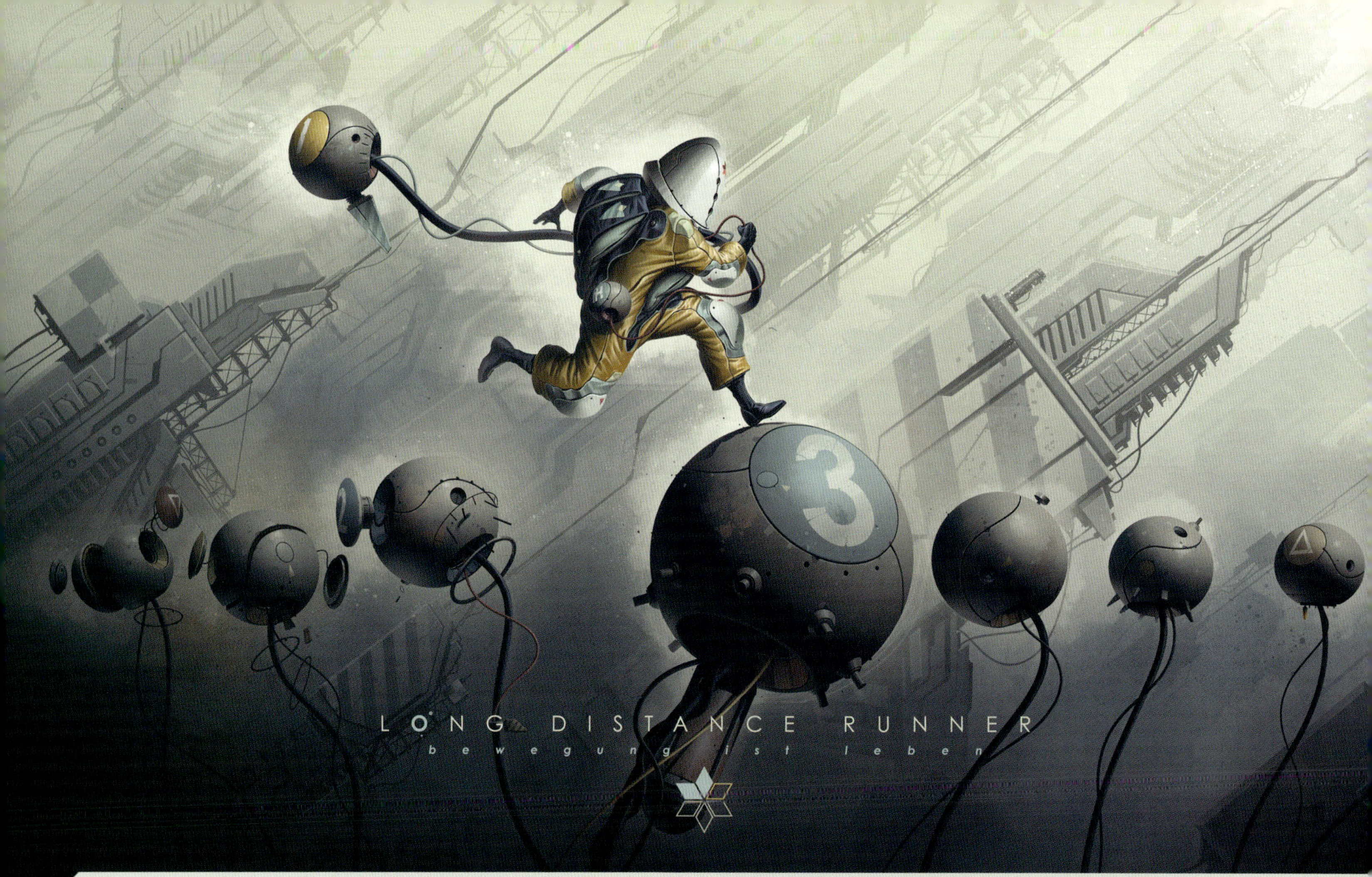

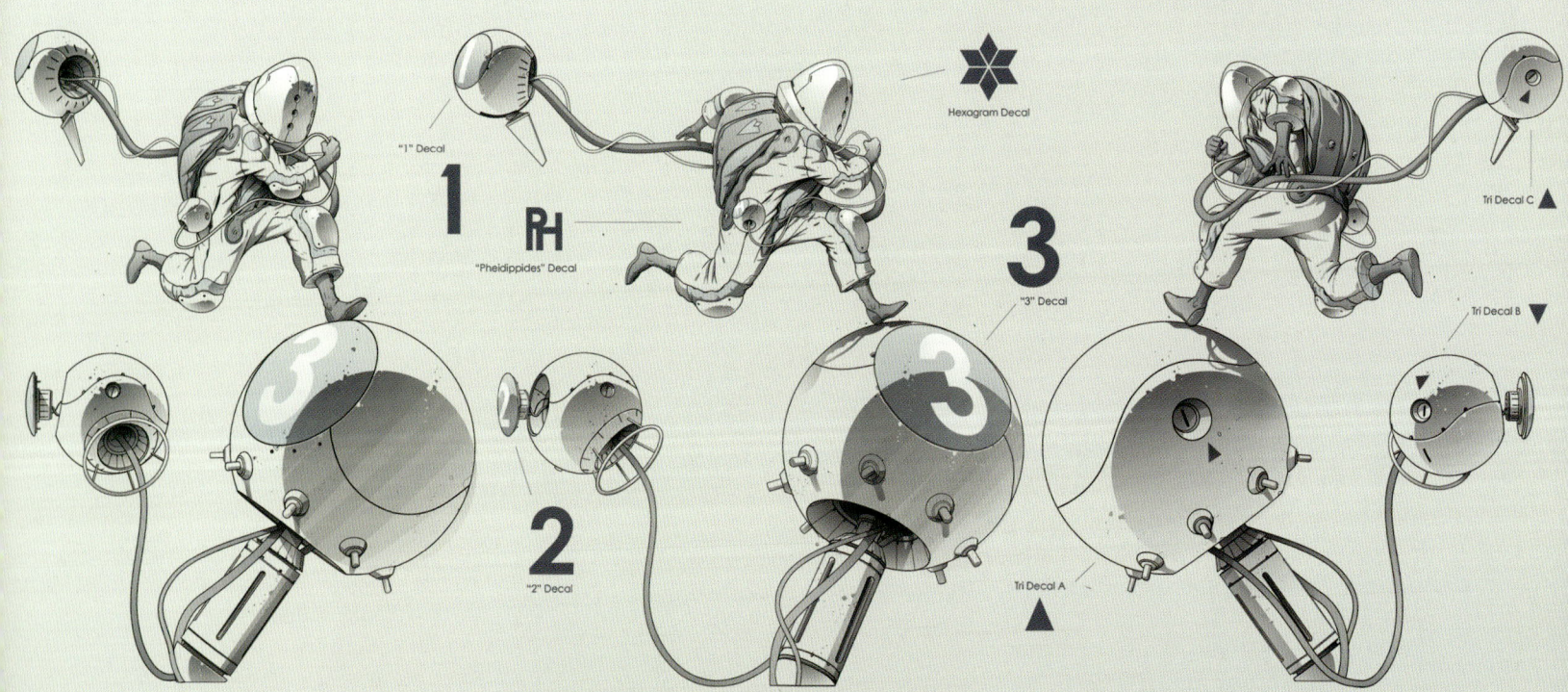

LONG DISTANCE RUNNER
bewegung ist leben

Decals -
Decal call out examples are not to scale.
See Decal Vector sheet for final design and decal colour info.

Hexagram Decal

1 "1" Decal

RH "Pheidippides" Decal

3 "3" Decal

Tri Decal C

Tri Decal B

2 "2" Decal

Tri Decal A

Front 3/4

Profile

Back 3/4

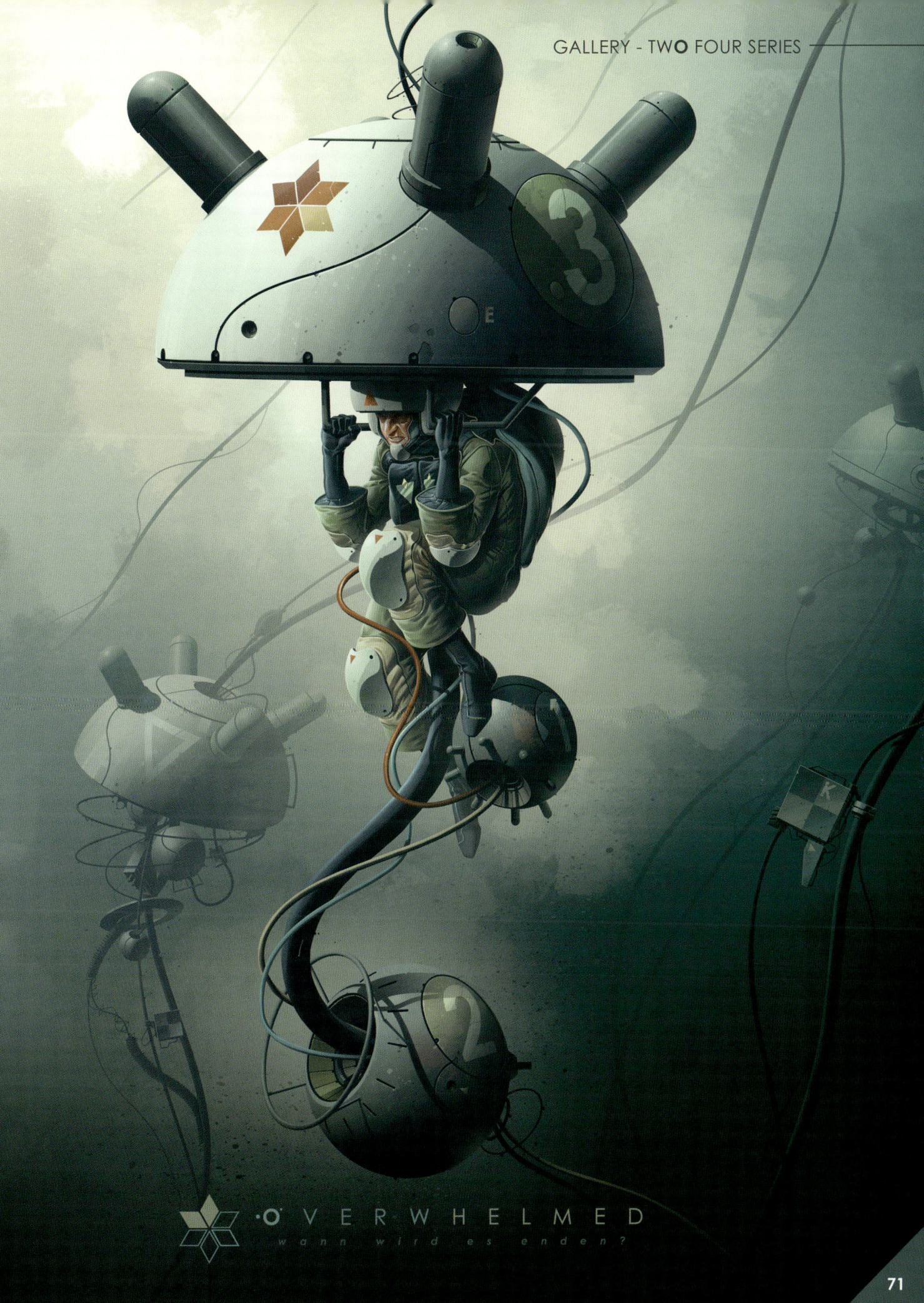

OVERWHELMED
wann wird es enden?

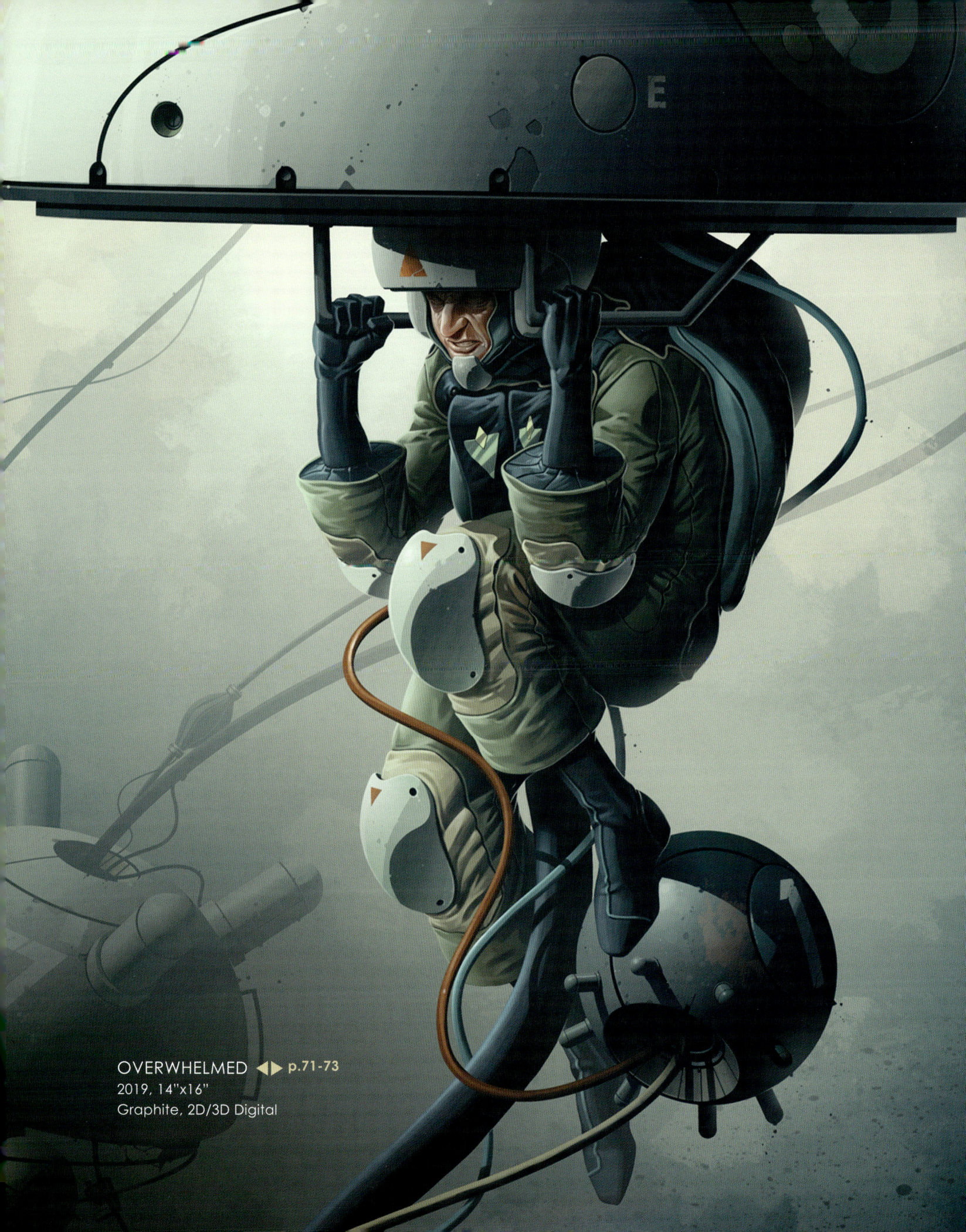

OVERWHELMED ◄► p.71-73
2019, 14"x16"
Graphite, 2D/3D Digital

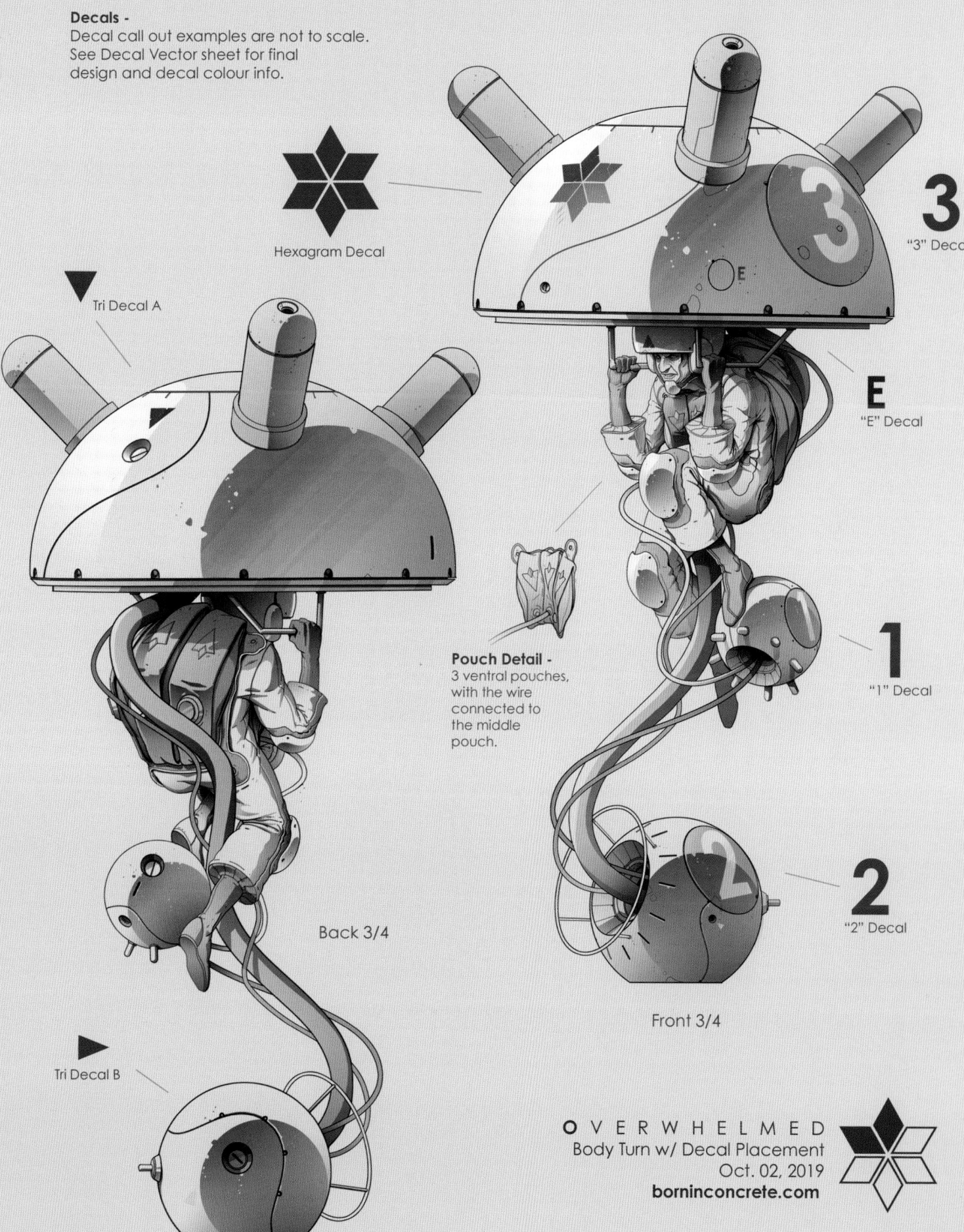

Decals -
Decal call out examples are not to scale.
See Decal Vector sheet for final
design and decal colour info.

Hexagram Decal

Tri Decal A

"3" Decal

"E" Decal

Pouch Detail -
3 ventral pouches,
with the wire
connected to
the middle
pouch.

Back 3/4

"1" Decal

"2" Decal

Front 3/4

Tri Decal B

O V E R W H E L M E D
Body Turn w/ Decal Placement
Oct. 02, 2019
borninconcrete.com

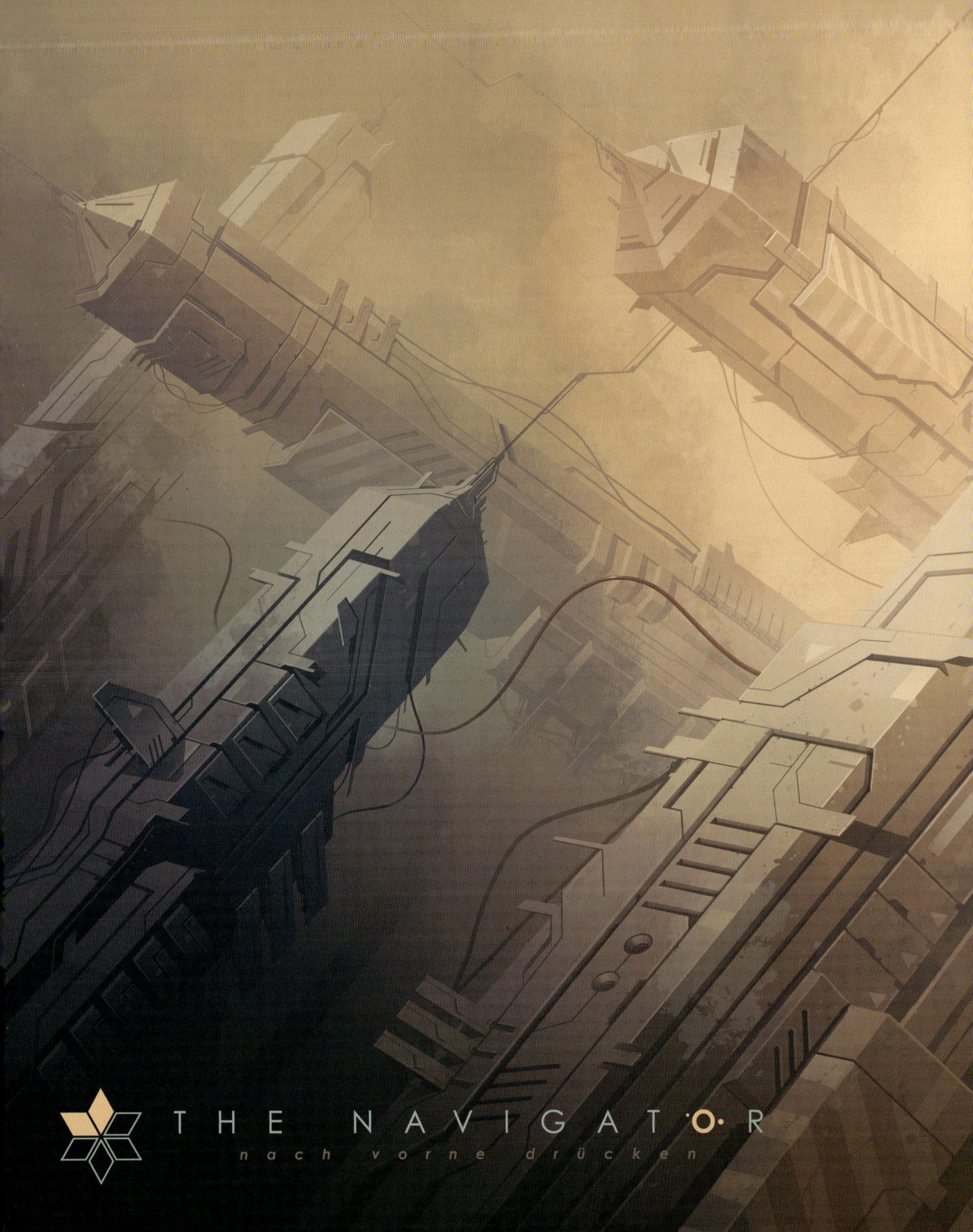

THE NAVIGATOR
nach vorne drücken

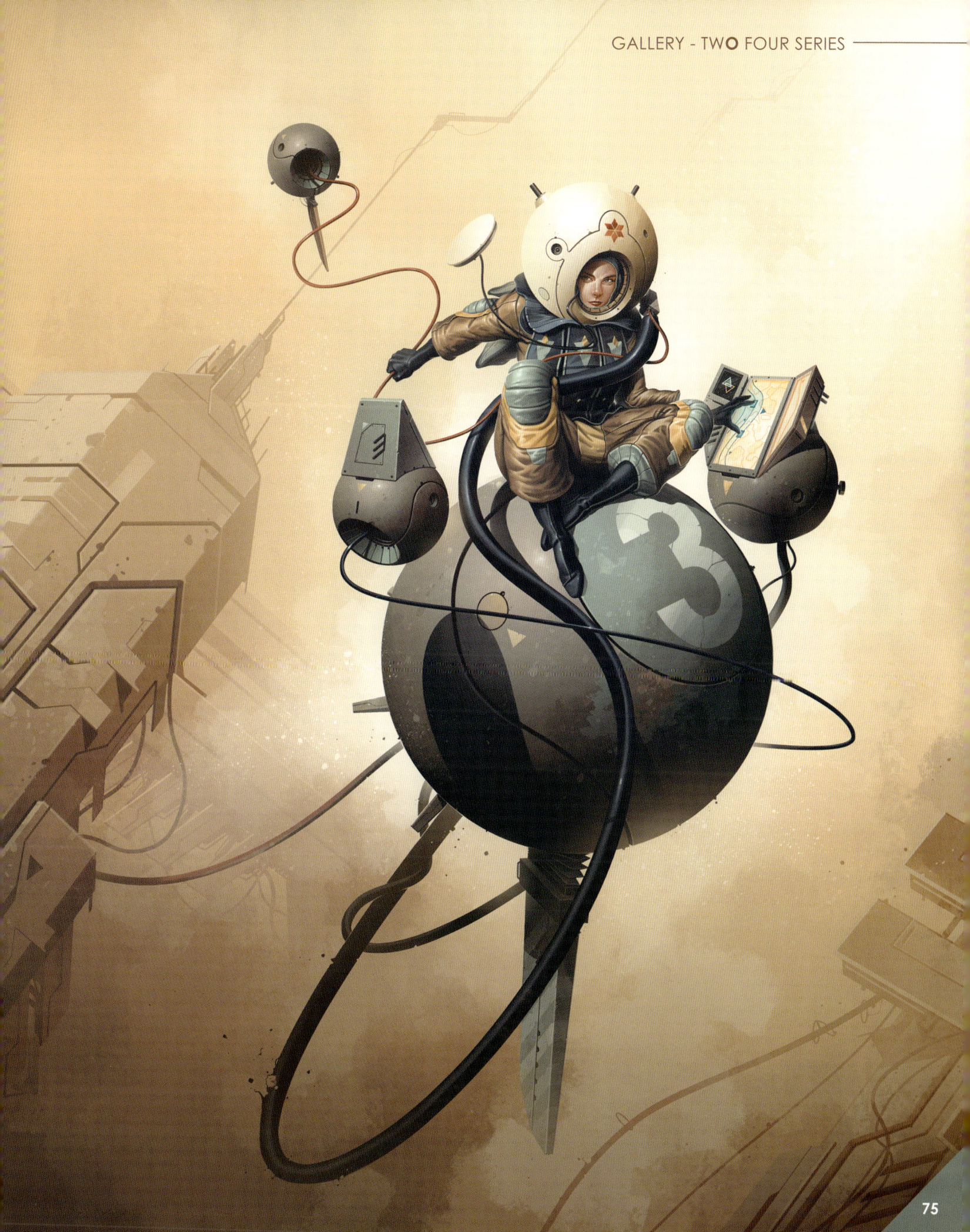

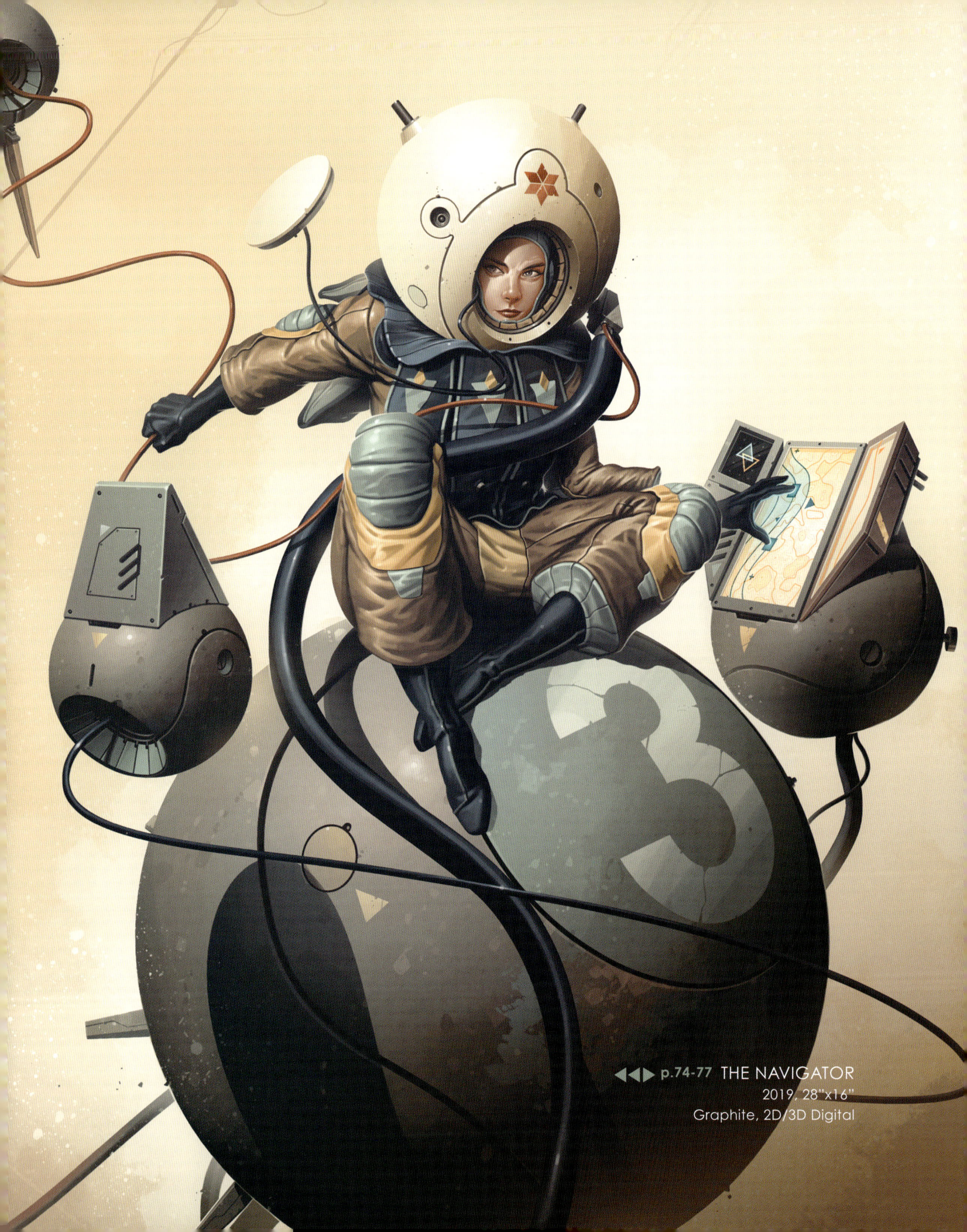

◄◄► p.74-77 THE NAVIGATOR
2019, 28"x16"
Graphite, 2D/3D Digital

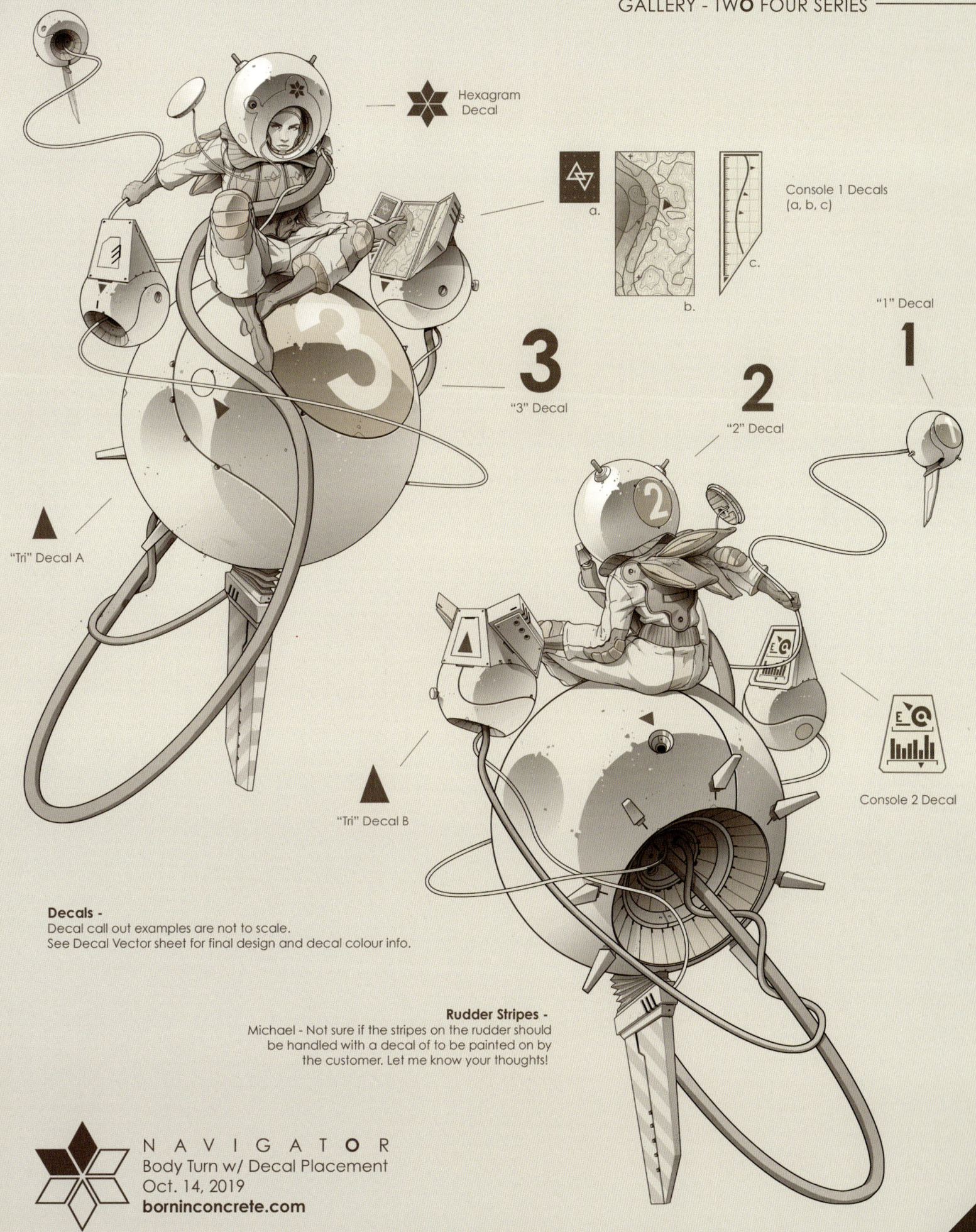

Hexagram Decal

Console 1 Decals (a, b, c)

a.

b.

c.

"1" Decal

3
"3" Decal

2
"2" Decal

1

"Tri" Decal A

"Tri" Decal B

Console 2 Decal

Decals -
Decal call out examples are not to scale.
See Decal Vector sheet for final design and decal colour info.

Rudder Stripes -
Michael - Not sure if the stripes on the rudder should
be handled with a decal of to be painted on by
the customer. Let me know your thoughts!

N A V I G A T O R
Body Turn w/ Decal Placement
Oct. 14, 2019
borninconcrete.com

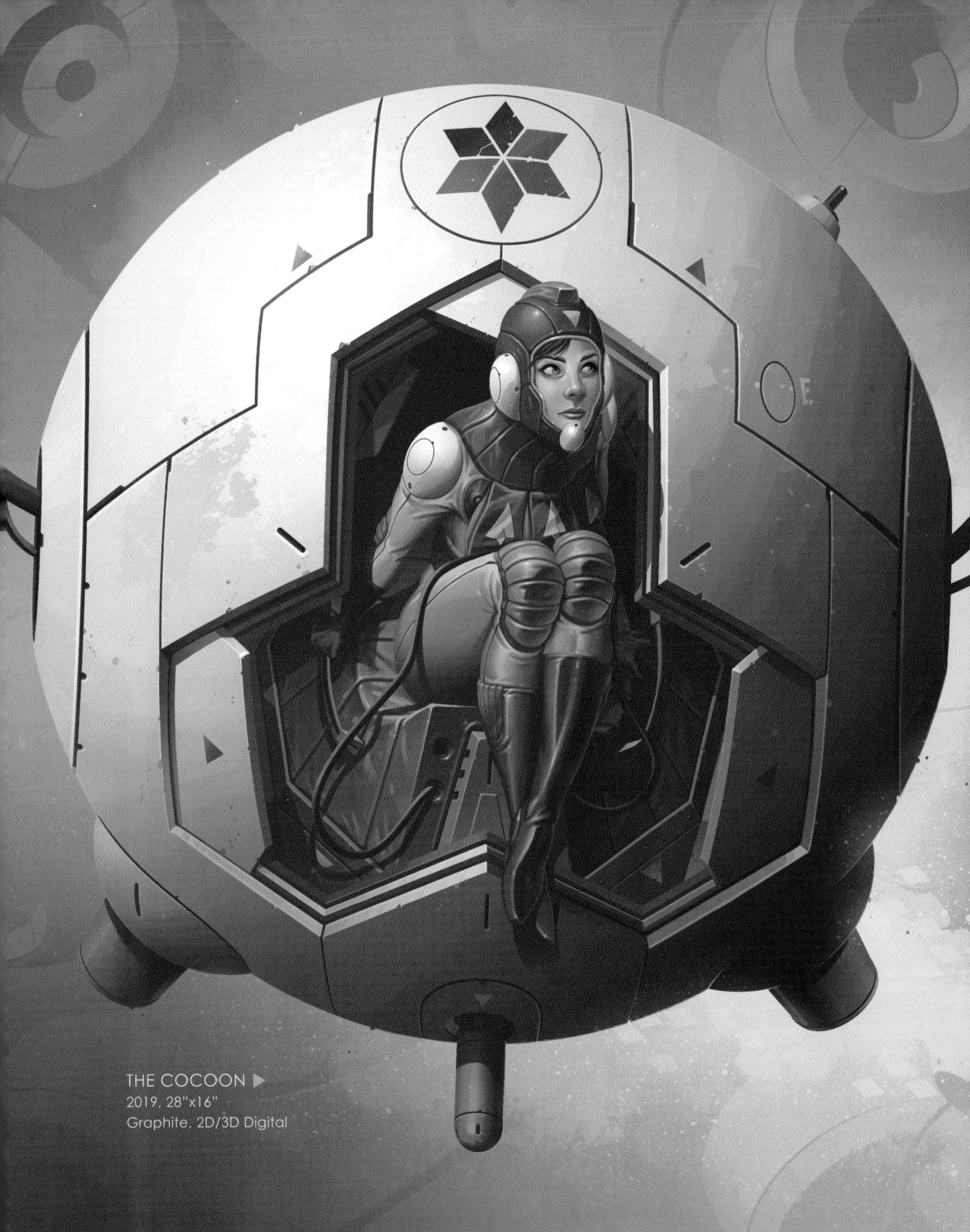

THE COCOON ▶
2019, 28"x16"
Graphite, 2D/3D Digital

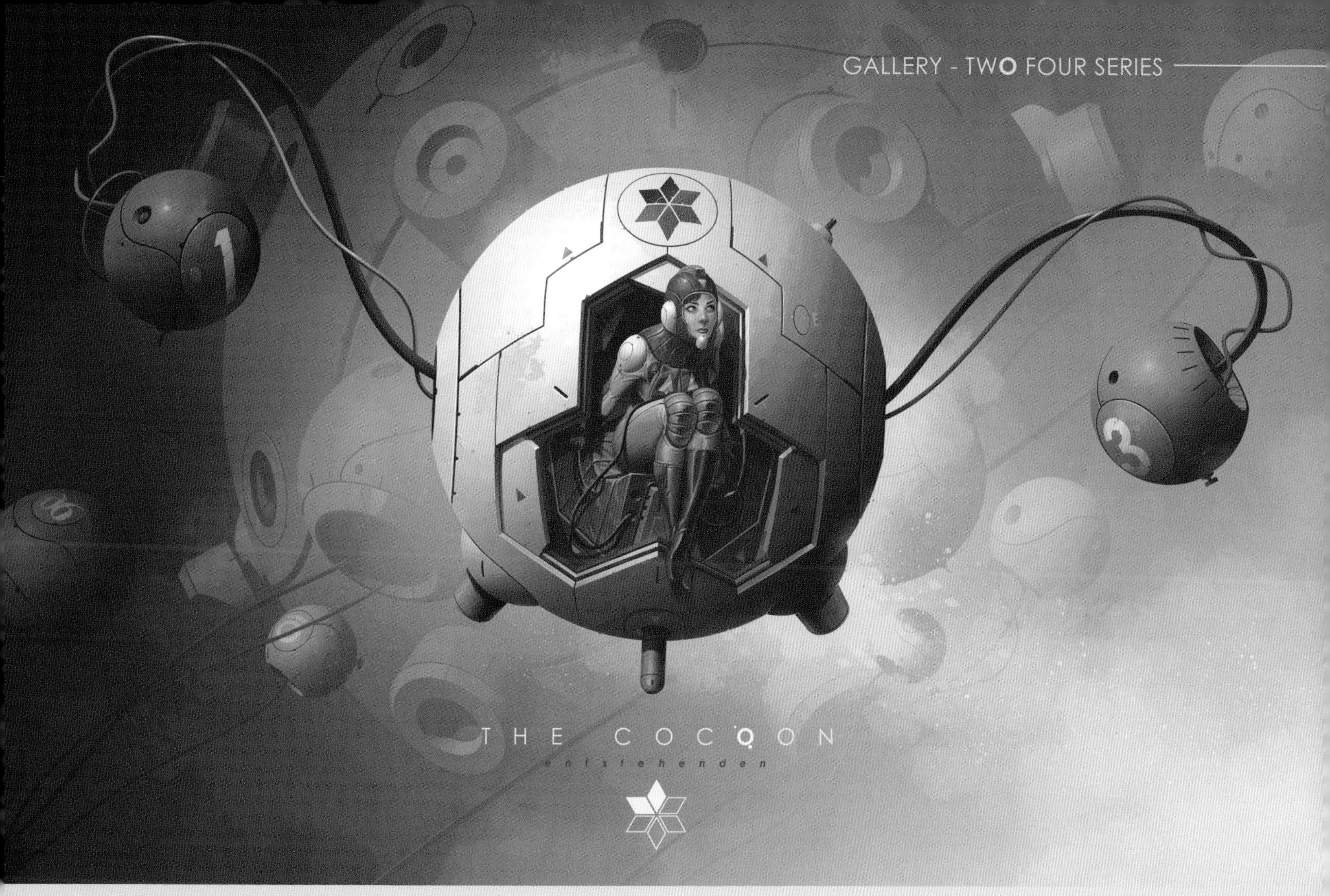

THE COCOON
entstehenden

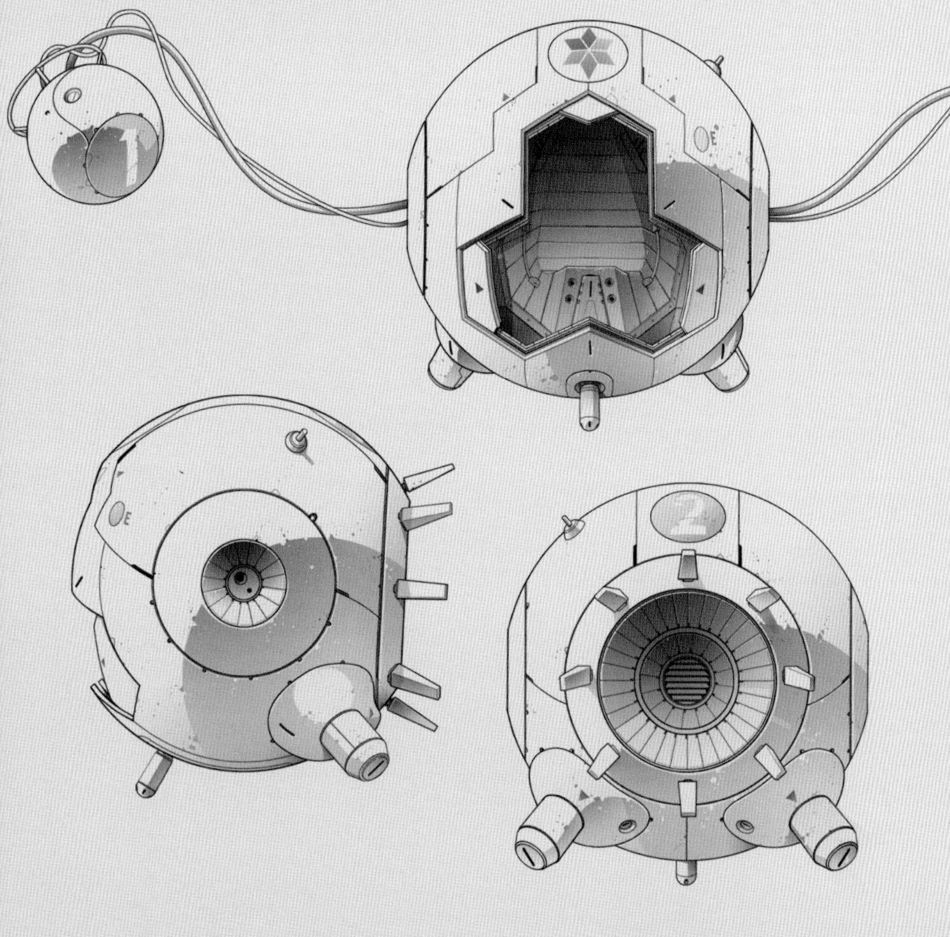

cont. from p.68

Fast forward to late summer of 2021. Michael at Industria Mechanika contacts me wanting to revive this project. Ever the creative entrepreneur, in the past year he has reinvented a large portion of his business to focus on 3D printable downloadable model kits. This effectively bypasses all the shipping and production problems he was dealing with.

The talented Leo Haslam that I had worked with on the Traveller project was brought in to do the sculpting. I'm happy that these pieces will finally see the light of day in a way that they were originally intended to.

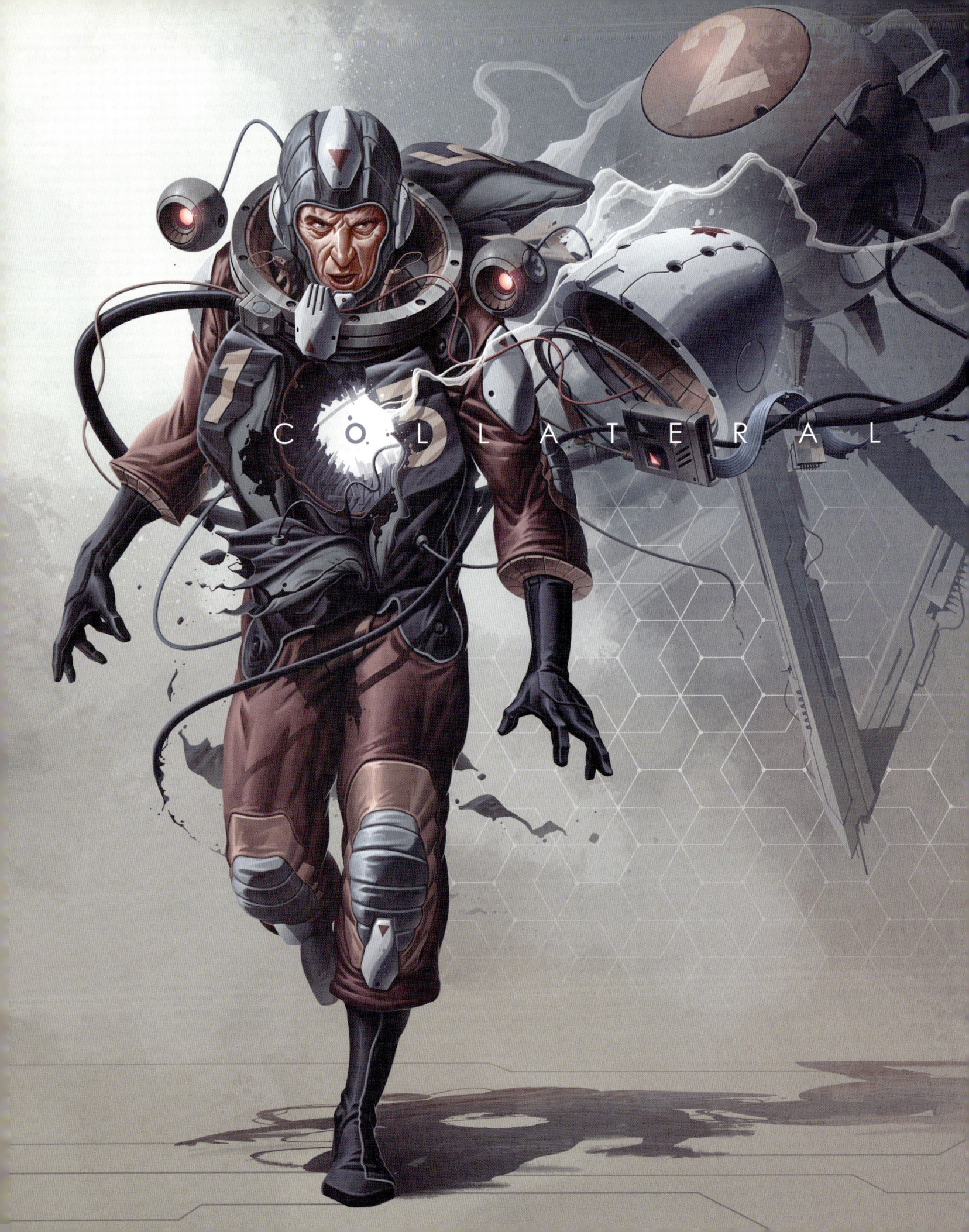

COLLATERAL

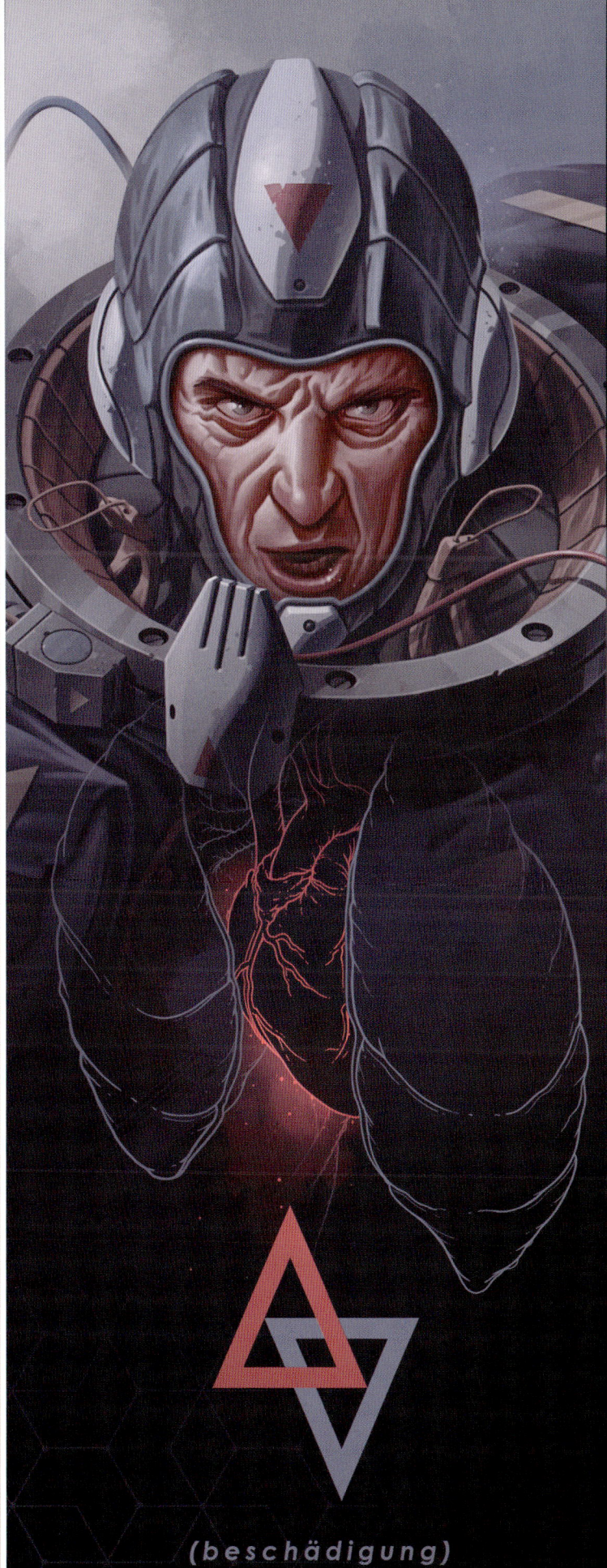

(beschädigung)

◄ COLLATERAL *(damage)*
2021, 18"x 15"
2D/3D Digital

Things can sneak up on you. After most of the stress and difficulty during these last few years had passed, I thought I was doing fine. But once everything calmed down, that's when the chest pain started. Various medical tests indicated that there was nothing wrong with me physically. And while the pain eventually passed, I'm left with the idea that I have some emotional and mental stuff to work through, or I need to get another opinion!

TAKE YOU AWAY FROM HERE
▶▶ p.82-83
2021, 16"x 20"
Graphite, 2D Digital

By the summer of 2020, my dad's dementia had reached an advanced stage. His body was there, but his mind was not. The care facility was doing their best to look after him, but lack of contact with me during the three-month-long Covid-19 quarantine had quickened his decline. I was finally able to visit him again by early summer 2020, but due to Covid restrictions, these visits were limited to an hour once a week. I would visit him in the hope of seeing a glimpse of his former self, but I never got one. The man I knew and loved had faded away.

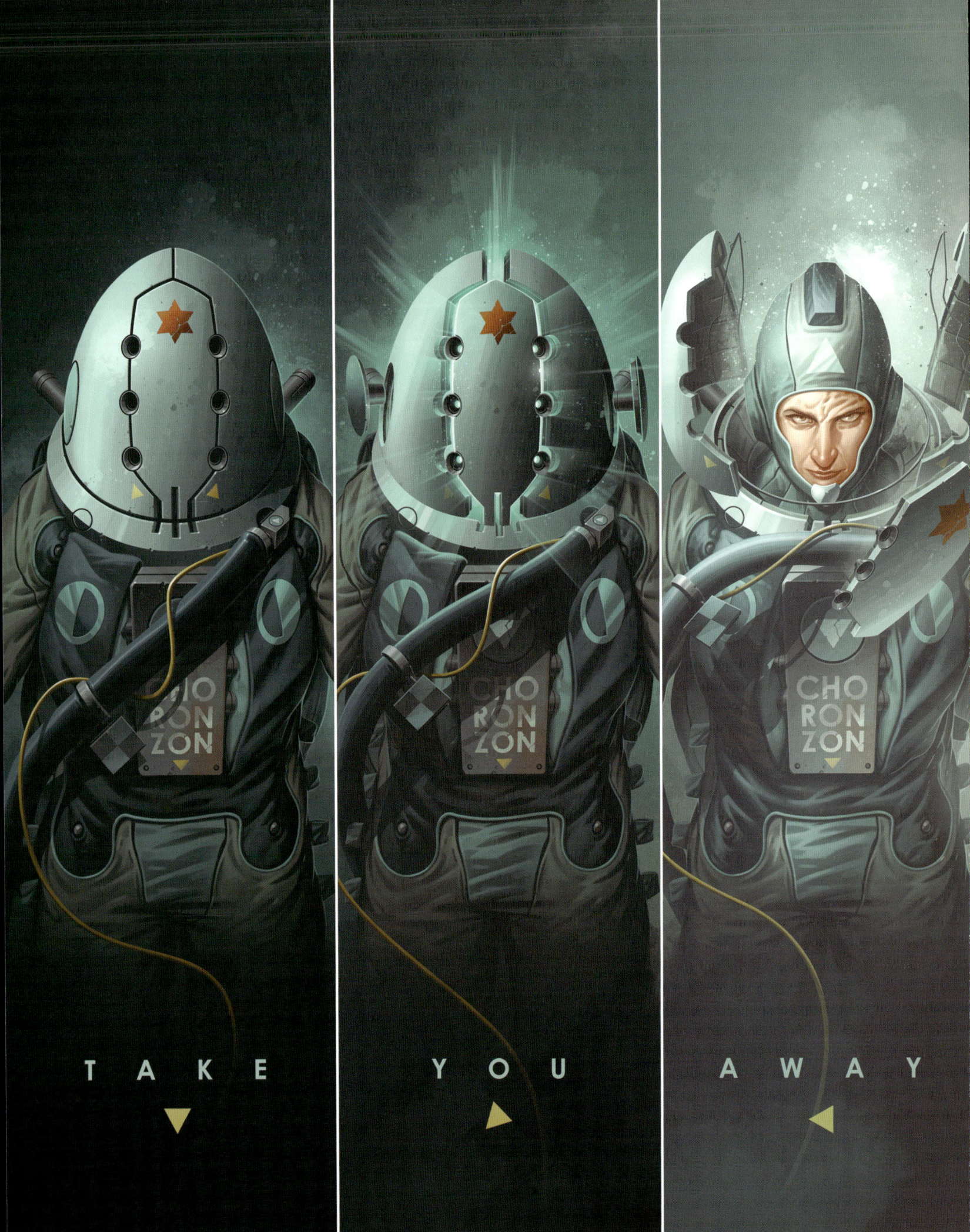

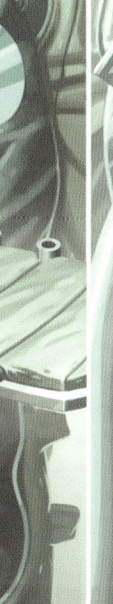
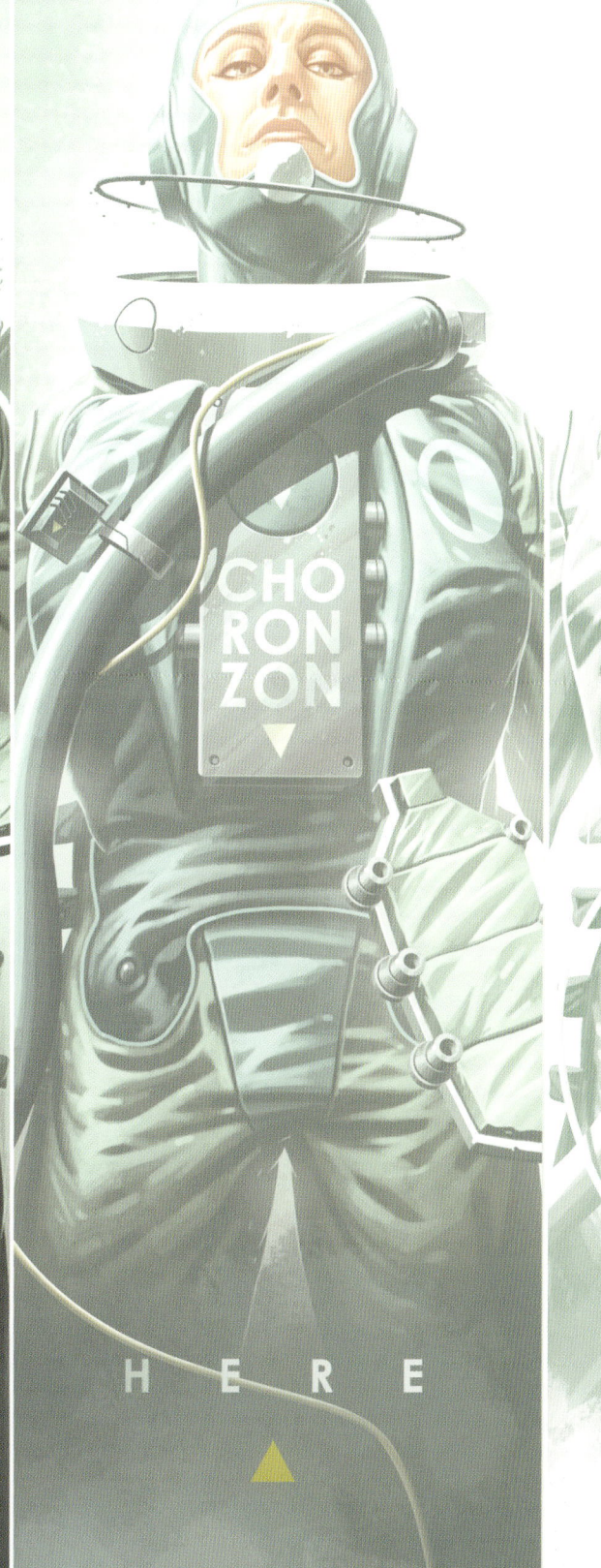
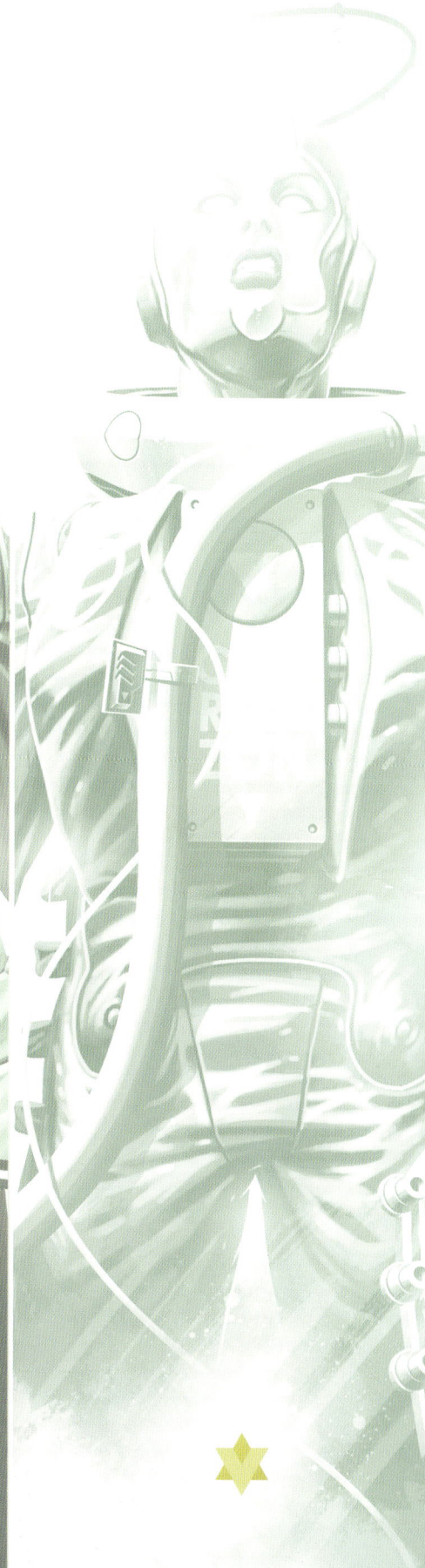

CHO RON ZON

CHO RON ZON

FROM

HERE

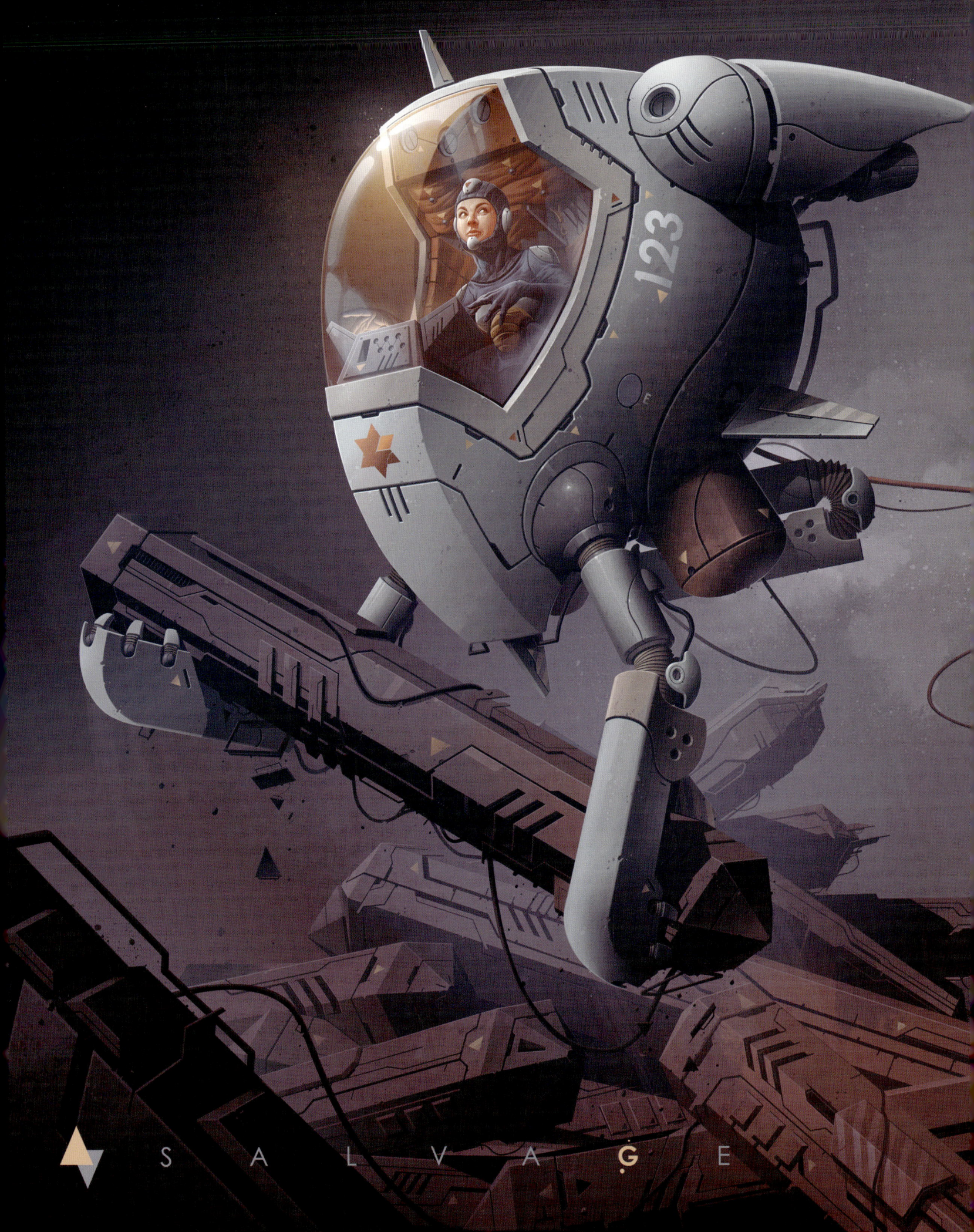

SALVAGE

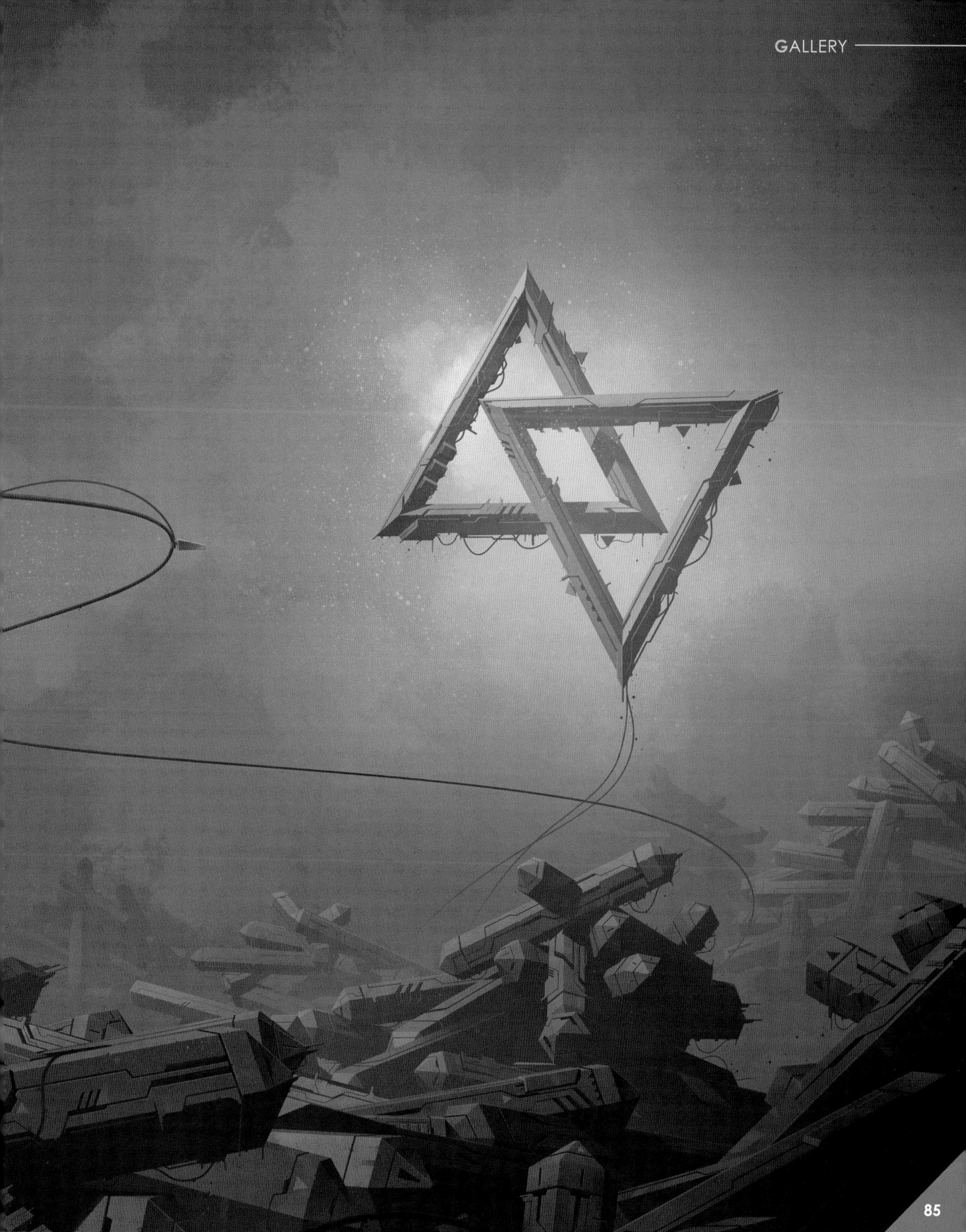

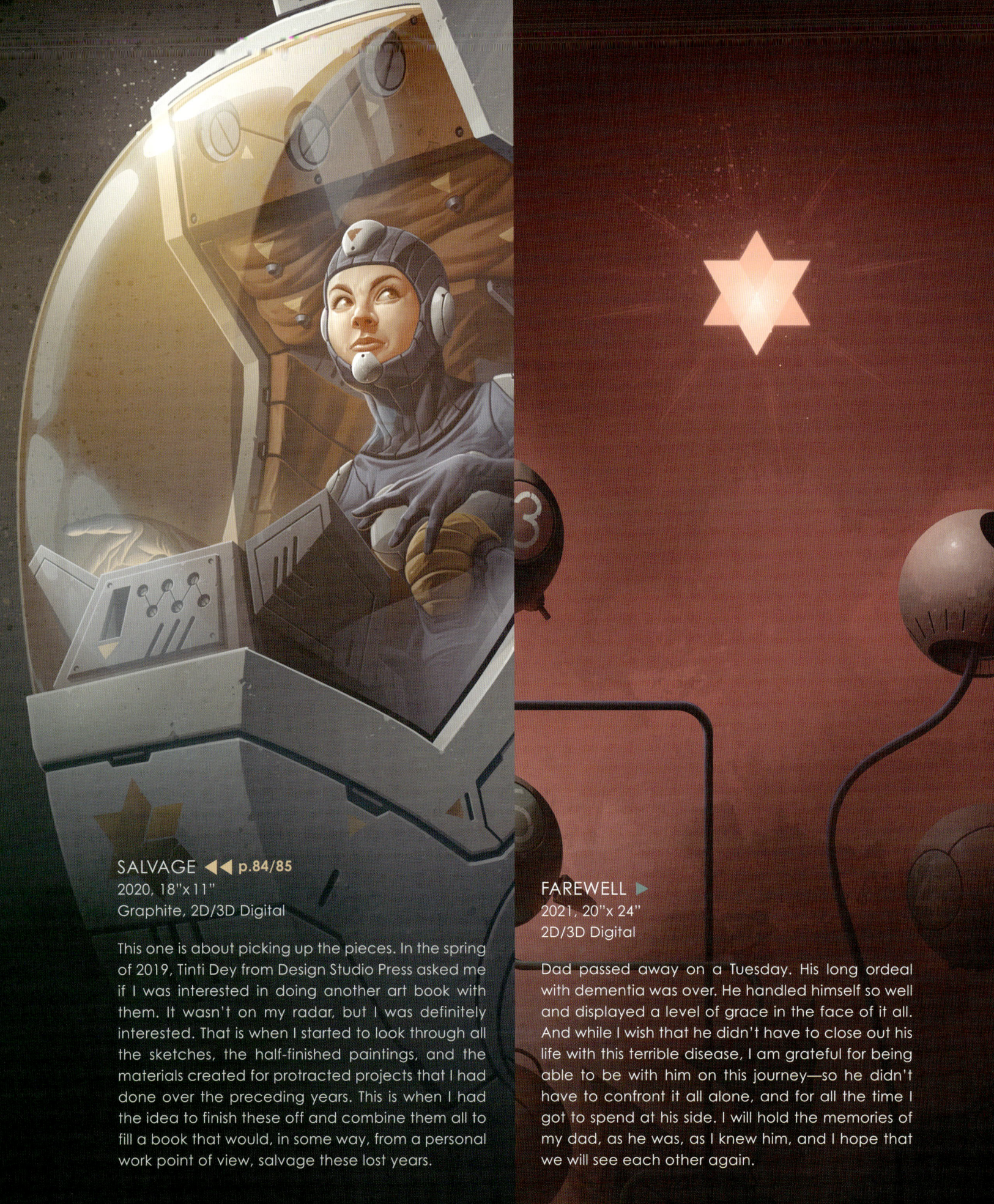

SALVAGE ◄◄ p.84/85
2020, 18"x11"
Graphite, 2D/3D Digital

This one is about picking up the pieces. In the spring of 2019, Tinti Dey from Design Studio Press asked me if I was interested in doing another art book with them. It wasn't on my radar, but I was definitely interested. That is when I started to look through all the sketches, the half-finished paintings, and the materials created for protracted projects that I had done over the preceding years. This is when I had the idea to finish these off and combine them all to fill a book that would, in some way, from a personal work point of view, salvage these lost years.

FAREWELL ►
2021, 20"x 24"
2D/3D Digital

Dad passed away on a Tuesday. His long ordeal with dementia was over. He handled himself so well and displayed a level of grace in the face of it all. And while I wish that he didn't have to close out his life with this terrible disease, I am grateful for being able to be with him on this journey—so he didn't have to confront it all alone, and for all the time I got to spend at his side. I will hold the memories of my dad, as he was, as I knew him, and I hope that we will see each other again.

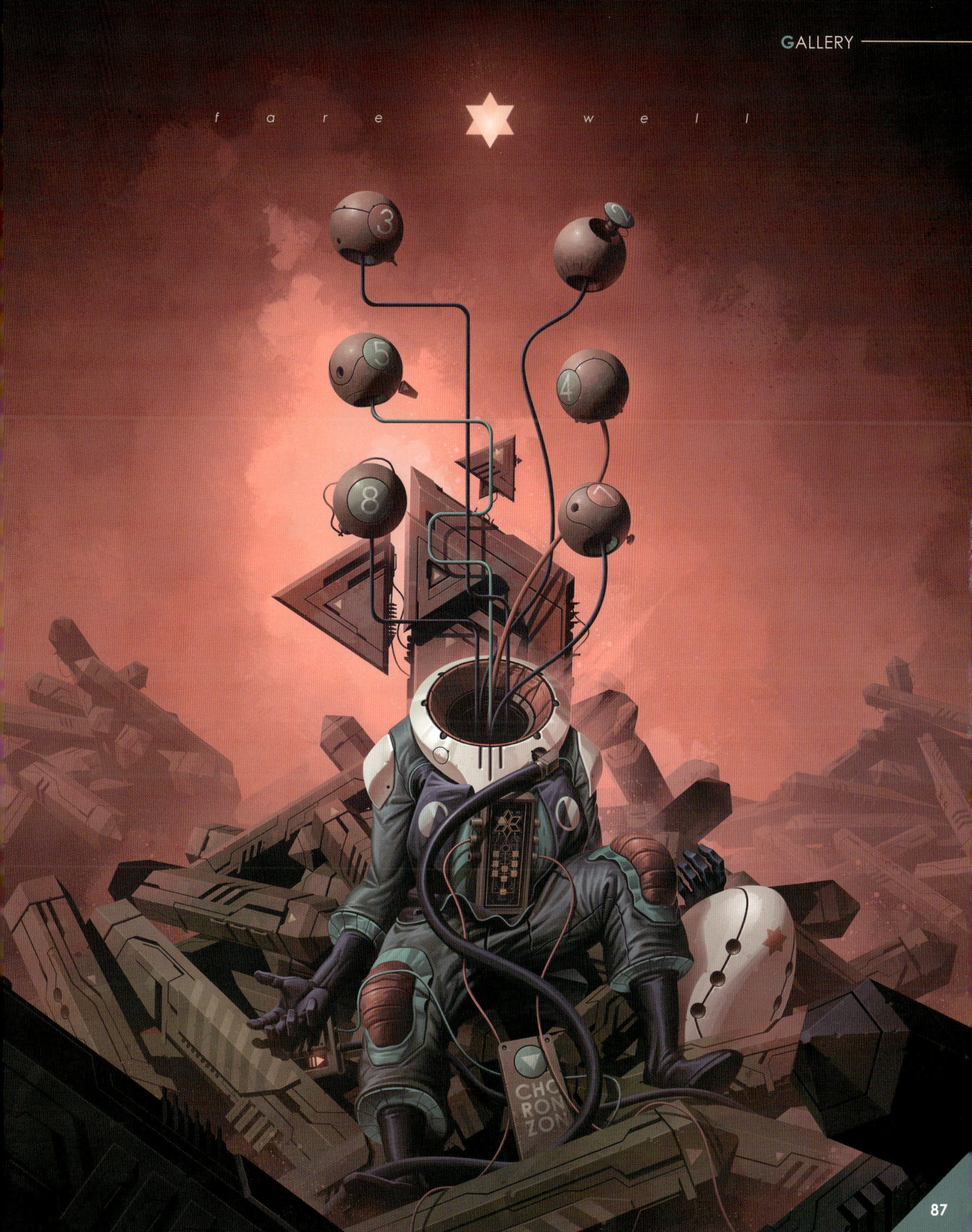

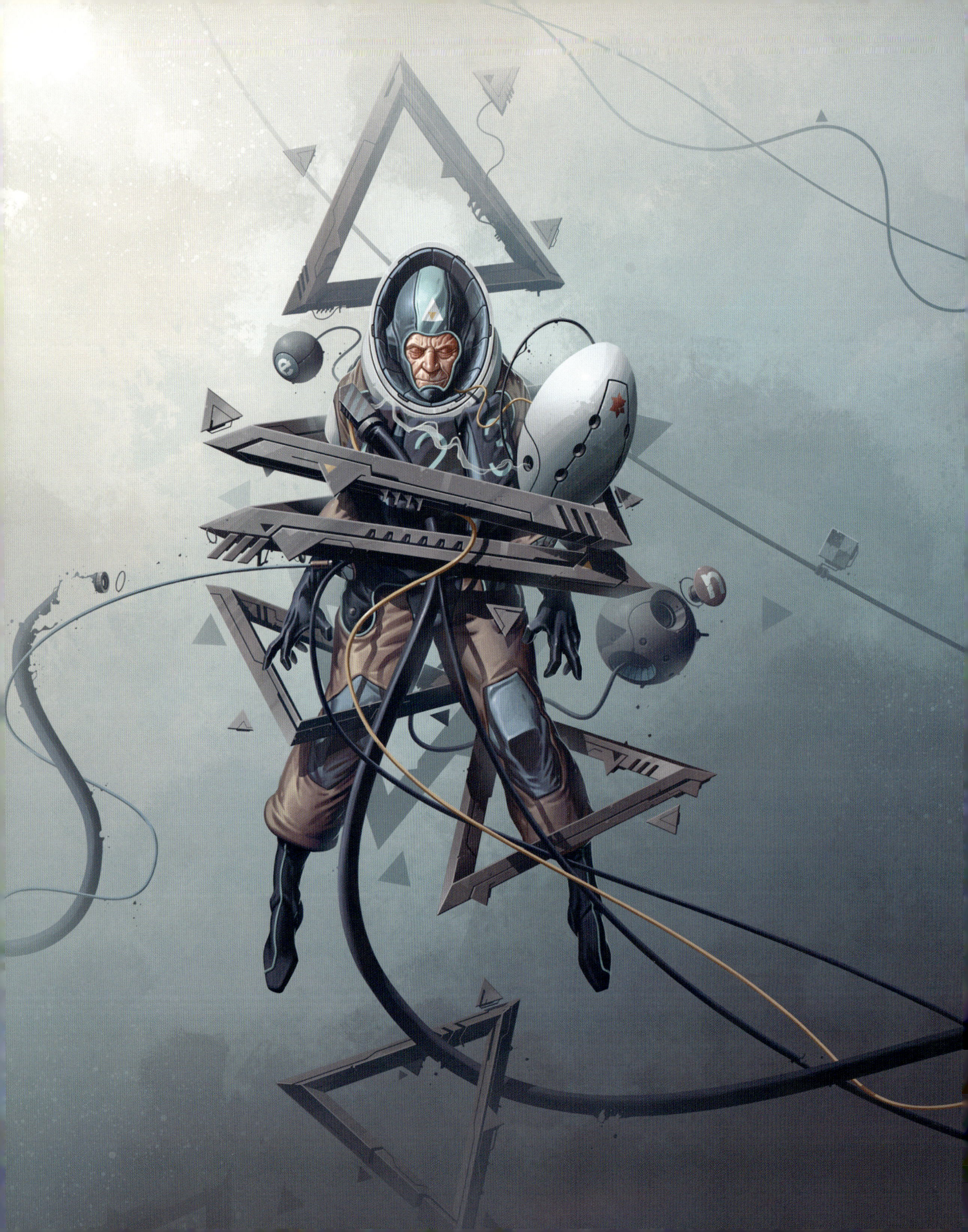

EPILOGUE

At the time of this writing, it has been more than two and a half years since I embarked on the journey to finish off this second EK Series. I had wanted to finish it up sooner, but I got sidelined a few times along the way. My family's heath and well-being during a global pandemic, as well as being at my father's side during his long hospitalization and his eventual passing, took priority over this project. Big thanks to Scott and Tinti at DSP for being so understanding when I pushed out my book deadline on more than one occasion.

I'm also grateful that during this time, the long, drawn-out collaborations like the Duchess and the Traveller eventually launched and were ultimately successful. Even elements of the Two Four series will see the light of day, albeit in a different form than originally planned. I consider myself very lucky to have these talented, creative collaborators that want to take this work in new, different directions.

My work situation also changed during this period, and thankfully I no longer need to have multiple projects going at the same time. Hopefully this will allow more regular time to work on new personal projects. Time will tell.

cont. p.91

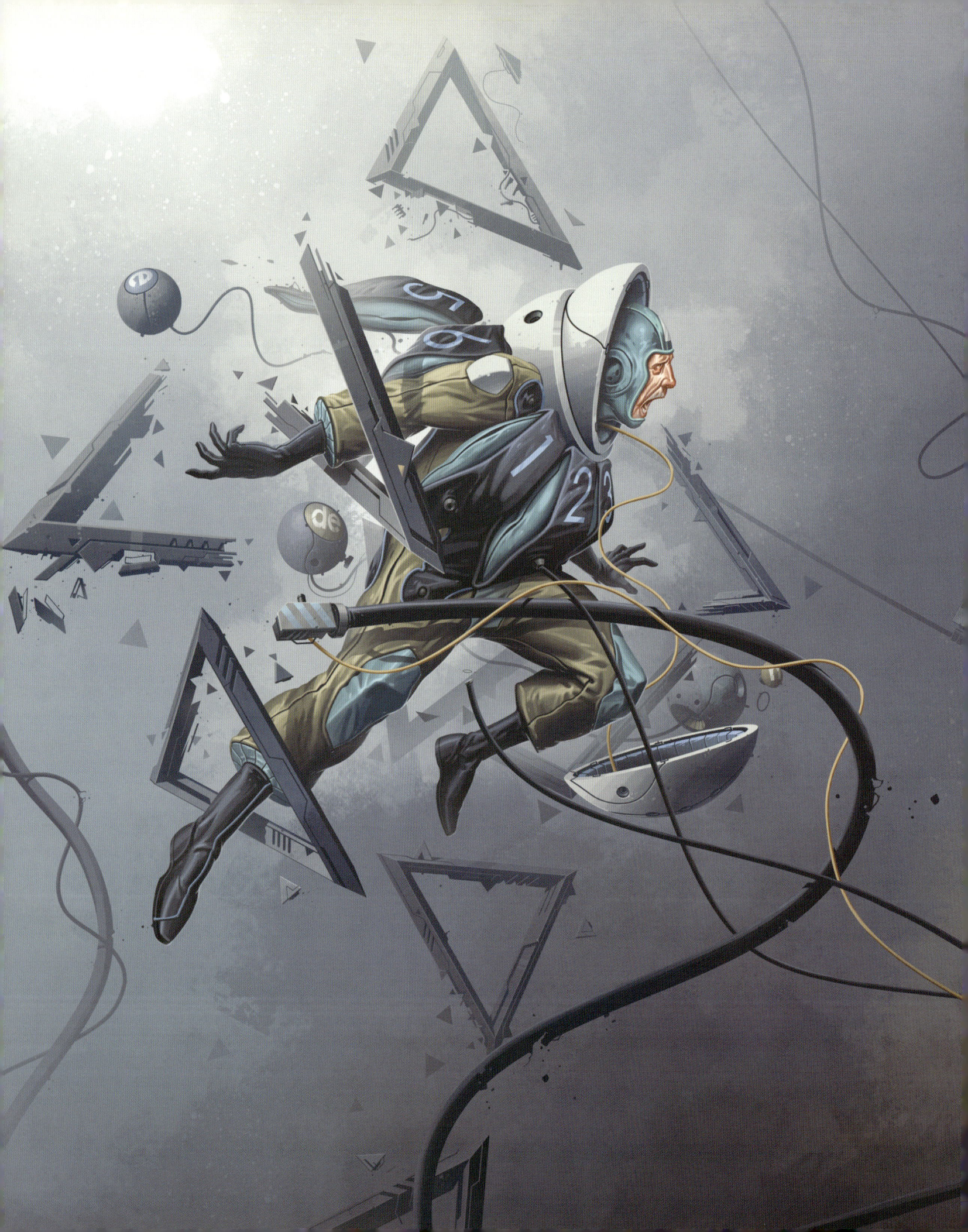

cont. from p.89

As for the work itself, this second EK Series rejuvenated me creatively in a way, just as the first one did. As I mentioned in the introduction, during the lost years the sketches and half-finished pieces allowed me to blow off steam and distracted me from all the stuff going on in my life. During the last couple of years, I have found that the process of going through this old work to finish it off has given a sense of artistic meaning to those years, and as I had hoped, has also given me a sense of closure. It has also reminded me that maintaining my own creative vision, my own personal projects, is an important part of my creative well-being. It was also a lot of fun, and I hope you enjoyed it as well.

See you on the next one.

Derek Stenning
2022

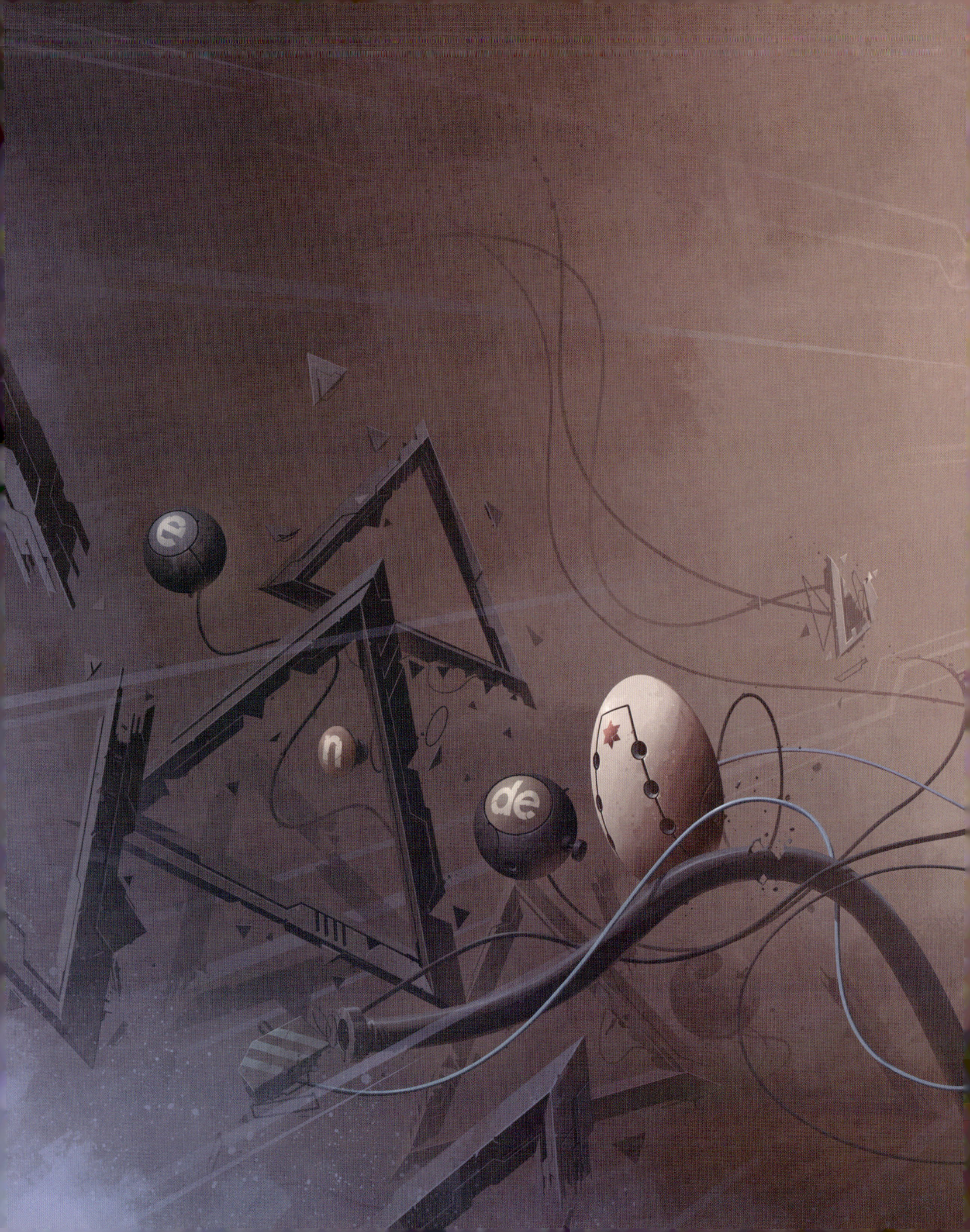

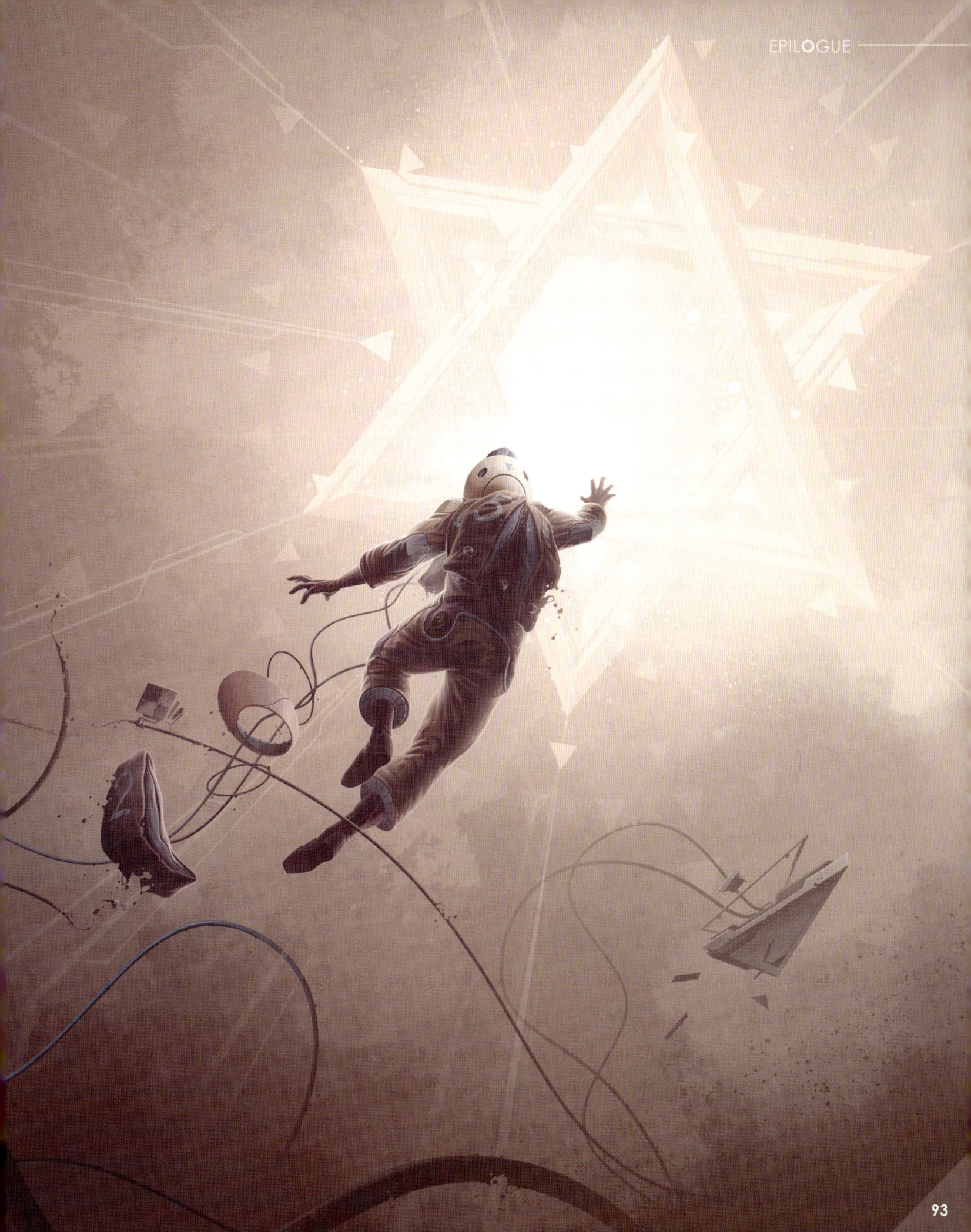

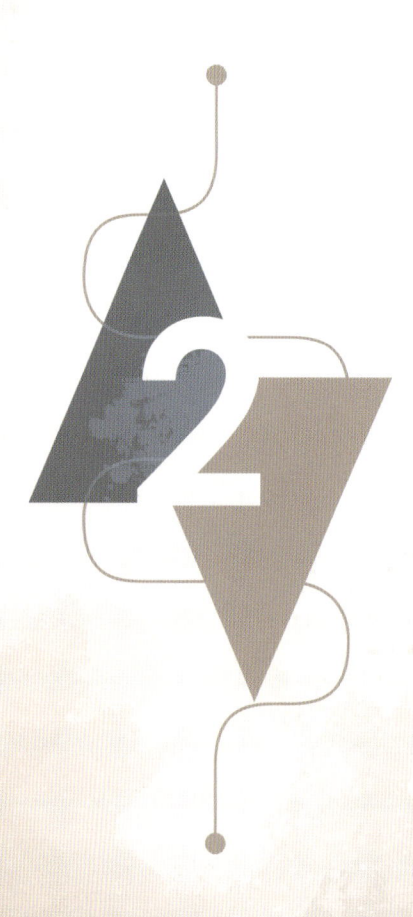

DEREK STENNING

Trained as a traditional animator, Derek is a concept artist and illustrator working in the game development field. Over the years he has worked on projects for companies like Nintendo and Microsoft, as well as titles for several independent studios and smaller start-ups. He is currently a concept artist at Next Level Games.

His personal project, Entartete Kunst, or the EK Series, was undertaken to get back to his creative roots. This project has been translated into numerous other forms, including book/magazine cover art, limited edition art prints, and a line of resin model kits, to name a few. This is his second EK art book, following ***Born in Concrete: The EK Series***, also published by Design Studio Press.

Derek lives in Victoria, BC, with his wife and two kids.

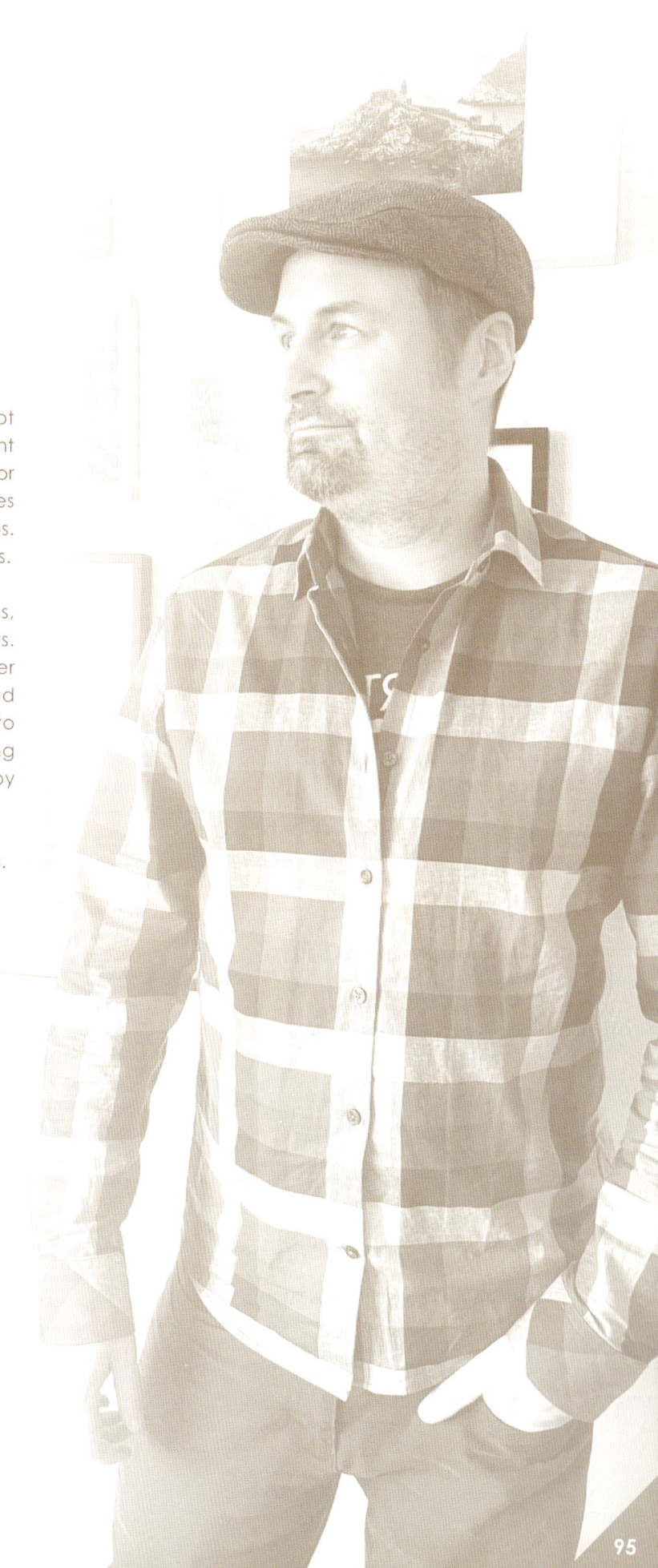

ALSO AVAILABLE

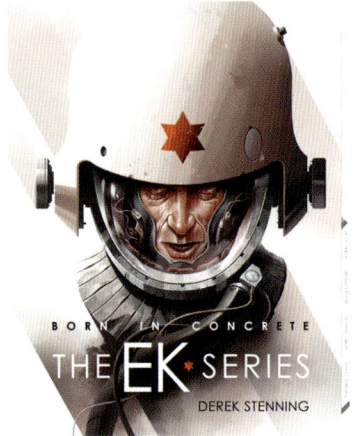

Born In Concrete: The EK Series
2nd Edition
96 pages
9"x 11"
Hardcover

This book chronicles the first EK Series, created by Derek to get back to his creative roots. Also includes design materials from several collaborations and a step-by-step tutorial.

Published by Design Studio Press

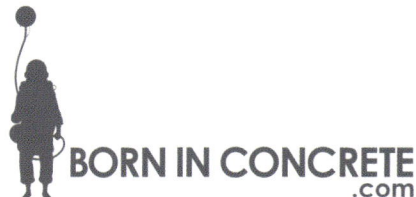

Limited edition prints, signed copies of art books as well as the latest news regarding Derek's art can be found at: **borninconcrete.com**

For EK statues, paintable maquettes, The Traveller Design Werks art book and other EK-related items available from Ax2 Limited, please visit **a-x-2.com**

industria mechanika

3D printable model kit files featuring designs from the EK Series are available from Industria Mechanika at: **industriamechanika.com**